I0790808

A Wilderness Adventure

Canoeing, Camping and Fishing

in

Quetico Provincial Park

A Memoir

By

William Monger

A Wilderness Adventure

A Wilderness Adventure

Canoeing, Camping and Fishing

in

Quetico Provincial Park

A Memoir

ISBN: 978-1-6884-5601-3

For Mary Jane - my wife, my best friend and my biggest cheerleader. She's put up with a lot over the last 52 years! Without her unwavering love, support, and encouragement, I would likely be six feet under, or my ashes scattered to the wind by now.

"I sit in happy meditation on my rock, pondering, while my line dries again, upon the ways of trout and men. How like fish we are: ready, nay eager, to seize upon whatever new thing some wind of circumstance shakes down upon the river of time! And how we rue our haste, finding the gilded morsel to contain a hook. Even so, I think there is some virtue to eagerness, whether its object prove true or false. How utterly dull would be a wholly prudent man, or trout, or world!"

-    Aldo Leopold, "A Sand County Almanac"

Prologue

I've been writing this memoir in my head for more than thirty years. Often, I would think about the trip I had taken to the wilderness of Canada's Quetico Provincial Park with three buddies. Parts of it are still so fresh in my mind that I can still smell the clean, crisp morning air, the pungent smoke from a campfire, hear the loon's plaintive call on a calm evening and see the Milky Way as I stared into the heavens on a chilly, crystal clear, night.

One evening this past winter, I was in my basement workshop cleaning up after a project and came upon a cardboard box that had been forgotten under a workbench for God knows how many years. It was full of "stuff" I rarely if ever used, but apparently couldn't seem to part with either.

I brought the dusty box up out of its dark cubbyhole, placed it on my assembly table, and pulled the string of my fluorescent shop light. I sat on a stool and opened it to find a used tack cloth, a plastic bottle of dried-up wood glue, a rusty putty knife, a glass cutter (I have 3 or 4 of them now because I can never find one when I need it), a couple of scraps of walnut and oak I kept just because they were beautiful, and one of those old folding rulers I had inherited from my dad. All of it was covered in shop dust from years past.

At the bottom of the box was a small spiral pocket journal and a folded topographic map, well-worn on the creases, and covered with coffee stains. It was the journal and map that I had carried with me on that Quetico adventure back in 1981, when I was 36 years old and in the prime of my life.

I carefully unfolded it and spread it out on the big table under the harsh light. The folds and edges were tattered and worn, it bore notations in pencil as well as a long, wandering line in a sort of figure eight, drawn in ballpoint pen, showing the exact route we had taken on that 8-day odyssey.

I traced the route with my finger, and then opened the journal to find cryptic notes from the trip. Most bore the simple headings of Day 1, Day 2, etc.

I became so totally engrossed in reliving that trip that I was startled when my wife came up behind me to say she was going to bed. It was nearly 11:00 pm and I'd been sitting there for well over two hours. I showed her what I'd found, and she suggested that maybe it was time I wrote that book I'd always talked about. Well, this is it, pieced together from my journal, my map, and my memories.

This is how I remembered it.

The Call

The call came unexpectedly one evening in early May. I had just moved my family into a new home that we'd watched being built since the previous October. On the phone was an old high school friend that I hadn't heard from in years. We'd been very close in those days, classmates, and workmates during summers on a local golf course grounds crew. We'd each married our high school sweethearts, who were also close friends.

We'd lost touch over the years as we went our separate ways. After college and law school, Tom had settled in not too far from where we'd grown up in the suburbs of Chicago. I'd gone to a different college, spent four years in the Air Force, gotten married, gone back to another college to finish an undergraduate degree, then made two job moves before finally settling in Southeast Michigan. There was no beating around the bush. After a few pleasantries, Tom asked, "How'd you like to go on a camping and fishing trip to Canada?"

"Wow, are you kidding me?" I replied. "Does a bear shit in the woods?!" I would confirm later that bears actually DO shit in the woods.

He explained that he and his two brothers-in-law and another friend had been going to Canada's Quetico Provincial Park every summer for the last eight years. This year, the other friend had a conflict and couldn't go. Tom knew that I'd been a fishing nut for most of my life and asked if I was interested in filling out the foursome this year.

Having just moved into our new house the month before, I was up to my eyeballs in projects, like grading, planting grass, trimming trees, and building a deck, not to mention working full time and helping my wife, Mary Jane, raise two sons who were a very active eight and four. Still, I'd thought about a trip like this for years, but always felt it was a little beyond my reach.

I'd heard of the Boundary Waters Canoe Area and Quetico but had never been there and knew little about it except for where it was located, straddling the U.S. - Canadian border north of Ely, Minnesota. I'd also never set foot in a canoe before, having done most of my fishing from 12 or 14-foot fishing boats with outboard motors, but how hard could it be?

After discussing details like dates, logistics, and costs, I told Tom I'd give him an answer in a couple of days. That night, Mary Jane and I sat down and talked about it. Tom said the trip was already planned for the first week in August and we'd be in the wilderness for eight days. Apparently, the dates were firm because park quotas fill up quickly and they had to make reservations early. The park's entry points were restricted and allowed only a small number of campers to enter each day. The entry point Tom and his buddies always used was on the Canadian side of Lac La Croix, and only allowed two parties per day to enter the park. This was to prevent ecological damage to the park as well as to preserve the wilderness experience for visitors. We would spend the first night at a motel in Ely, where we'd pick up our supplies and backpacks from the outfitter. Mary Jane urged me to go, suggesting that another opportunity like this might never come up. She's selfless like that.

Playing devil's advocate, I pointed out that I'd be gone for ten days, eight of which would be in the wilderness with no means of communication should an emergency arise at home. This was 1981, well before GPS, the internet, cell and satellite phones. At that point, she began to worry about *me*. "What if someone gets hurt or sick? How do you call for help in the middle of nowhere?" she wondered. Giving that some thought, I replied, "I guess one guy would have to stay behind with whoever got hurt while the other two would paddle back to civilization for help." This really was going to be a wilderness experience. There are no resorts or settlements of any kind in Quetico, and likewise, no cabins, stores, motorboats, airplanes, or even regular patrols. This was remote canoe country! It was possible that we wouldn't even see another human being from the time we left the ranger station on Lac La Croix until we returned eight days later. Mary Jane figured she would be fine, having plenty of friends close by, and her parents living a mere 20 minutes away. And so, it was settled... I was going!

The next evening, I called Tom back and told him I was in and began to pepper him with questions about everything; from food to fishing gear, tents to canoes, and clothes to critters. I needed to start preparing. He laughed and said they'd been doing this for years and had it down to a science. The main thing to keep in mind was that while you had to bring enough to be self-sufficient, you also had to carry everything you brought. He said, "And there will be portages." I asked, "What the hell is a portage?"

He explained, "When you go from one lake to another, sometimes there's not a connecting river, and you have to carry the canoes and all of the gear from one to another. Also, there are places where there *is* a connecting river, but the rapids are too dangerous, or there's a waterfall you need to go around." When I asked how long the portages were, he said, "They can be from a few hundred feet to a half-mile or more."

After a short pause, he added, "and you have to do every portage twice."

"What?" I asked. Patiently, he explained, "We'll have four guys, two canoes and six backpacks, plus fishing rods. That means two trips for each guy for each portage." Reality was beginning to set in. I needed to try to get myself into better shape! I had let myself get "a little soft."

I was in sales and covered a 4-state territory, so I spent a lot of time driving and flying, but not much time exercising. Luckily, our new house backed up to 5,000 acres of state land that was wooded and hilly, so I started hiking. I also did a lot of work around the yard and house, building my deck and thinning out the trees to let in some sunlight to get grass to grow. I had about two and a half months to go.

Preparation

Tom told me that over the previous eight years, they had tried lots of different approaches to these trips regarding supplies. What were essentials vs. what were luxuries?

On their first few trips, they had opted for freeze-dried camping fare to save space and weight, but had brought way too much in the way of clothing, jackets, blankets, etc. They also decided that even when supplemented with fresh-caught fish, the freeze-dried rations were not very palatable. "Actually," he said, "they sucked."

They had also gone to the other extreme of hauling in real food like bacon, eggs, ham, potatoes, flour, bread, butter, pancake mix, syrup, fresh fruit, peanut butter, Oreos and instant coffee. This was the era of Folgers freeze-dried coffee crystals, fresh from NASA!

All that stuff was bulky and heavy, but after eight years of trial and error, they had decided it was worth it, and much more enjoyable to pack in lots of real food to supplement the daily meals of fresh-caught fish. Paddling and portaging every day in the fresh Canadian air gave you a tremendous appetite. While packing in the real stuff made the logistics and the portages tougher in the beginning, it got easier each day because the packs got lighter as the perishables were, necessarily, consumed early on.

They had a 4-man tent, a Coleman camp stove with a small propane bottle, ropes, a tarp, a collapsible shovel (to bury your poop), but I would need to bring my own inflatable air mattress, a sleeping bag, rain gear and a couple of changes of clothes. We would wash our clothes in the lakes as we went. Everyone brought a small first aid kit. Each guy would have a personal backpack, and there would be two additional packs for the food, cooking and eating utensils, and camp ax, which would be rented from the outfitter, making for six backpacks in all.

I needed to choose my fishing gear carefully because I had to carry it on every portage, along with a camera, reading material, a journal, and a couple of rolls of toilet paper. Clothing must be well-thought-out, but Tom suggested at least one pair of jeans to go along with several pairs of shorts. There would likely be times when it was cool and windy. Rain gear would be essential since they had always encountered rain at some point. Three or four sets of underwear, a couple of sweatshirts or flannel shirts, two pairs of comfortable walking shoes (you always wanted to have one dry pair) and three or four pairs of socks. After eight years of doing this, they pretty much knew what worked and what didn't.

I had one additional requirement that the other three did not. I had to bring all my stuff onto an airplane because I had to fly commercially from Lansing to Duluth where they would pick me up on their drive up from Chicago to Ely.

I began to put some things aside that I thought I'd need to take along, and I spent some time going through my fishing gear, starting with the rods and reels. It would all be spinning gear. I chose three rods, one with reasonably stiff action, one with a medium action and one with ultralight action. Catching a big fish on ultralight gear was great fun!

I went through my tackle boxes, trying to decide what would be most effective in the waters we were going to fish. At Tom's suggestion, I chose mostly crankbaits, mainly in large to medium sizes that would run at varying depths. I also set aside some jigs and a couple of spoons. Finally, I re-spooled two reels with new monofilament line, one with 10 lb. test and the smaller one with 6 lb. test.

I had a pretty good tubular rod case which I'd need in order to take the rods on an airplane in checked baggage. Before putting the rods in their case, I inspected them to be sure the ferrules were solid, the line guides didn't have any nicks that would wear on the line, and that the thread windings were solid and not frayed. These were little things I did routinely when I fished local bass tournaments. Five years before, six friends and I started the first B.A.S.S. chartered bass club in the area, the Michigan Bassmasters. It had grown to about fifteen members by 1981 and is still active today.

This trip was not going to be just about fishing. It was also about adventure, exploration, camaraderie, and enjoying the beauty of unspoiled nature. Still, I couldn't just dismiss the excitement of catching lots of fish!

Over the next month or two, as I prepared for the trip, I kept in touch with Tom to ask questions as they came to mind. "What kinds of fish do you catch most often?" (Walleye, Smallmouth Bass, Northern Pike and Lake Trout). "Have you ever had a problem with bears?" (No, not yet). "Do you guys always go to the same places on the same routes?" (No). "How warm or cold does it get in early August?" (High 80's to low 40's). "Have you ever seen a moose?" (No, but we keep hoping to). "Is it hard to find good campsites?" (No). "Have you ever capsized a canoe or had a serious injury? What's the plan if someone gets hurt?" Not surprisingly, he said they'd never had a bad injury but the plan, if they did, was what I had discussed with Mary Jane. One guy would stay back, and two would paddle out for help. They'd had a couple of capsizings, but luckily, they had been in shallow water, and nothing had been lost.

Black bears are numerous in the Boundary Waters Canoe Area (BWCA), and Quetico, and while bear encounters are fairly common, they apparently are seldom dangerous. According to a 19-year BWCA study, there had only been two serious injuries reported due to bear contact in nearly 19 *million* visitor-days. Still, precautions needed to be taken when storing food. They were also cautious on longer portages. There were wild blueberry patches along some of the portage trails, and blueberries are a delectable treat for bears (as well as for campers), so it encouraged us to make noise during our treks from one lake to another.

The route they had planned would cover some familiar water but would also take a new path into some lakes they'd never before visited. This year they planned to go as far as Conmee Lake which they'd never done. That would take us about 30 miles, as the crow flies, from the drop-off point. In canoe miles, it would likely be closer to 40 or 50.

Having been a Geography major in college, I had a good collection of atlases. I studied the area as best I could, but detail was lacking. This was twenty plus years before Google Earth was invented. I needed a more extensive scale map than any of my atlases provided, so I wrote to the U.S. Geological Survey to see if I could get a topographical map of the area. Apparently, the USGS could provide maps of the U.S. side with a little bit of overlap, but not what I was looking for. I did some calling around southeast Michigan to find a store that specialized in maps, atlases, globes, etc., and found one that had a few topo maps, published by the Canadian Dept. of Energy, Mines and Resources out of Ottawa.

I look back today and marvel at the ease with which we can now do this sort of research compared to 1981. With just a few mouse-clicks, you can now find out more in a few hours than you could by doing months of dedicated research just a few decades ago. Still, I wouldn't trade that experience for the world, as that extensive preparation ultimately made the trip much more rewarding. I discovered that nowadays, nearly every visitor carries a GPS receiver and you can even rent satellite phones from outfitters when you head out.

Even after several months of research combined with my trip mates' experience, there were still a lot of unknowns coming our way. Many decisions would need to be made on the spot. The weather could, and probably would, impact a lot of our travel plans, and the weather would be an unknown. We would get a local forecast in Ely the night before we launched out of Lac La Croix, but from that moment on, we'd be on our own and at the mercy of whatever Mother Nature had in store for us. Tom said they'd never had a trip that was completely free of rain, nor had they ever had one without at least a few sunny days.

As the weeks passed, and the end of July was approaching, I found myself feeling stronger, with more stamina. I had shed almost ten pounds that I wouldn't have to carry with me on those portages. I was excited for August to come!

Getting There

The night before I left home, I double checked my gear against my checklist. There had been some disturbing national news bubbling up over the previous few weeks regarding the Professional Air Traffic Controllers Union (PATCO). They were threatening a nationwide strike, and President Reagan was threatening to fire them all if they went out. That could potentially cancel my flight to Duluth. If I did catch my flight and they went on strike while I was out in the wilderness, I wouldn't know it until we returned to Ely and possibly would not be able to get back to Lansing.

I had trouble getting to sleep that night as I kept going over everything in my head. What was I forgetting? Once I left, it would be too late. What if I missed my flight? What if PATCO went on strike before I took off? A million little doubts nagged at me.

I awoke the next morning, Saturday, August 1st, to beautiful sunshine and blue skies. I had been restless all night but got at least a few hours of sleep. Still groggy, I took a shower, shaved, got dressed, and then... smelled bacon! Mary Jane was putting on a feast for me and our boys, Jamie and Tim. Over breakfast, they hammered me with questions, asking mostly about how big the fish were in Canada. Jamie, the oldest, had once caught a 22-inch northern pike, but Tim had only caught a few small sunfish from his Granddad's pond. We kidded over breakfast, and I promised to catch a big one and take plenty of pictures. I also promised we would all go fishing together when I got home. I told them they had to be good boys and take care of their mom while I was gone.

Checking my gear one last time, I loaded it in the car. It was about an hour's drive to the airport, but to err on the side of caution, I allowed myself 3 hours. I was NOT going to miss this flight!

Arriving at the airport in Lansing, I parked in the long-term lot and carried my duffel and fishing gear what I estimated to be about 200-300 yards to the terminal. A pretty good hike. Then I tried to imagine "portaging" that distance through the woods, carrying a heavy pack or a canoe. "No problem," I said to myself, "I can do this." I was in far better shape than when Tom called ten or so weeks earlier and was determined that as the "greenhorn," I was going to pull my own weight, and not be a burden to my fellow explorers.

I checked my duffel and the heavy-duty tubular rod case that held the three rods I had chosen to bring. Even though I only packed two reels, I brought an extra rod, thinking I may need a spare if I should happen to break one. Airport security was minimal in those days, and after checking my baggage, I was free to roam the terminal. Though Lansing is the state capital, the terminal seemed unusually quiet. It was a Saturday morning in August after all, so maybe not so unusual. I had a couple of hours to kill, so I walked the terminal end to end, wandered around the gift shop, got coffee, read the newspapers, went outside and watched airplanes come and go, and contemplated what the next week or so had in store for me.

My eagerness to get underway made the wait seem like an eternity, but eventually my flight was called for boarding. I've had a lifelong fascination with flying and whenever I flew anywhere, I always tried to get a window seat and follow our progress, visibility permitting. This flight was only about half-full, so I chose a seat just forward of the right wing which allowed great visibility.

In order to follow along, I would try to identify towns, major rivers, lakes, and especially the interstates. This trip took us west-northwest out of central Michigan, crossing the Lake Michigan shoreline north of Muskegon, near Ludington. It was clear and beautiful, and I felt like I could see forever. Most people who are not familiar with the Midwest in general and the Great Lakes in particular, have no concept of the size and scale of these wondrous, freshwater treasures. Mary Jane and I had once taken some friends from the east coast to one of our favorite beaches on northern Lake Michigan. When we arrived, our friend, Anne, was astonished that she couldn't see the other side. "It's like the ocean!" she exclaimed.

About 10 minutes later (at 500 mph that's about 80 miles), as we crossed over the Wisconsin shoreline south of Green Bay, I could see the Door Peninsula disappearing into the distance to the northeast, off our right wingtip.

Then crossing over Lake Winnebago, I realized that on this track, we would likely fly very near Stevens Point, where I'd gone back to school after my stint in the Air Force and where Jamie, my first son had been born. During our four years there, I had done a lot of fishing in the northern half of Wisconsin. I was lost in nostalgia as Stevens Point appeared ahead. From 30,000 feet, I could pick out the University of Wisconsin where I'd graduated seven years earlier. So much had happened in my life since I last set foot on that campus, not the least of which was the birth of Tim, my youngest, who was now four. In 1974, we'd moved from Stevens Point to St. Charles, Missouri to start my first "real" career job as a Sales Engineer with W.L. Gore & Associates. We were only there for 9-

months when they moved us to Michigan to take over a more significant territory.

So many thoughts were running through my mind as my old home disappeared behind us. I lost track of our route as we continued to the northwest over the seemingly endless green forests of northern Wisconsin, and I began once again to contemplate what lay ahead over the next ten days or so.

I felt the plane reduce power, and before long, the flight attendant was announcing our initial descent into Duluth and asking for tray tables to be stowed and seats returned to their full upright position. We continued our slow descent north out over the western tip of Lake Superior before making a left turn for a landing to the west in Duluth. After we passed over the city and then the airport threshold, the wheels gently kissed the runway, and I was jarred back to the reality of where I was and wondered if the guys had arrived yet from Chicago. The flight attendant welcomed us to Duluth and announced the local time as 2:30pm. Having gained an hour going from the Eastern to Central time zone, I reset my watch while we taxied to the gate.

Duluth was not a big terminal in 1981, making for a pretty short walk to the baggage claim. As I turned a corner into the claim area, I spotted Tom sitting in a row of seats along a wall waiting. "Hey!" I said, "How long have you been here?"

"Only about 15 minutes." he said rising to greet me, "We tried to plan ahead so we'd be here at about your scheduled arrival time. I'm not sure how long we'd have waited if you were going to be late.

"Ha," I said, " ...then I guess it's a good thing I was on-time!" We shook hands, laughed, and slapped each other on the back. It was good to see him. It had probably been seven or eight years.

"Damn, I'm glad you could join us," he said. "We're gonna have a terrific time! We're going to some places we haven't been before. We've always wanted to go all the way up to Conmee Lake. You're gonna catch more fish than you can handle. We catch and release unless we need a walleye or two for dinner... or lunch. By the end of the trip, you'll be tired of catching fish!"

"We'll see about that!" I said. We continued chatting until the baggage arrived. My duffel and rod case had survived the trip. Wayne and Bill were parked at the curb, waiting for us. Introductions were made, my duffel and rod case were crammed in with the rest of the gear, and we were off to Ely.

"What time did you guys leave home this morning?" I asked as we were leaving the airport grounds. Wayne, who was driving, said "A little before 7:00. It's about an eight-hour drive to here, and we have a couple more hours to get to Ely".

Bill then said, "When we get to Ely, we'll stop by the motel, then check in with our outfitter and make sure all of the arrangements are okay."

"What kind of arrangements?" I asked.

Tom said, "Well, they'll have our park reservations, cooking gear and utensils, and our empty backpacks, which we'll have to load up tonight. We also need to buy Canadian fishing licenses, and they also made the arrangements for the floatplane in the morning that will take us across the border to the Lac La Croix ranger station where we'll go through customs and pick up our canoes. I'm also going to buy a new paddle while we're there."

"Don't paddles come with the canoes?" I asked.

He said, "Yep, they do, but they're heavy commercial paddles that can take a lot of abuse. I'm buying a thinner, lighter, curved paddle that works a lot better and is easier to handle." I was already on a new learning curve. I thought a paddle was a paddle... little did I know.

Driving north, we left civilization behind, and I marveled at the beauty of the pine, cedar, spruce, and tamarack forests of northern Minnesota. White birches, scattered in clumps, here and there, added contrast to the dense, green wall lining both sides of the two-lane blacktop. An occasional dirt road wandered away into the woods like a muddy brown river. Were these driveways? I wondered what lay at the end of those roads.

Houses and small cabins were few and very far between. There was an occasional run-down trailer. I wondered what it would be like to live here year-round. How would you earn a living? How far would you have to go for groceries or supplies? What are the winters like?

I guessed it would be a very stark existence, one that would suit a loner, someone that didn't socialize easily. You'd likely have to be a hunter, a fisherman, and certainly a problem solver. Someone that was comfortable with his or her own company and didn't mind living off the grid. I didn't see any power lines anywhere. As a kid, I read the whole series of Jeff White Northwoods Adventure books by author, Lew Dietz. Although those books were set in northern

Maine, I'd always imagined it to be precisely this kind of country.

As we started, once again, to see indications of civilization, I was slowly brought back to reality. Signs began to appear advertising outfitters, souvenir shops, motels, resorts and everything you would expect from a town that made its living from summer tourists and visitors to the Boundary Waters and Quetico. It was coming up on 5:00pm when we pulled into the gravel parking lot of our motel. It felt good to get out of the car and stretch our legs. It was still warm and sunny, but the air had a unique quality about it. It was fresh and pungent with pine. It smelled like the North and the adventure that awaited.

After checking in and getting our room keys, we got back in the car for the short ride to the outfitter. Sure enough, they had everything properly arranged for us. We picked up our park reservations, fishing licenses, cooking gear, and empty backpacks, (these were large, heavy-canvas backcountry packs) and were told to be at the seaplane anchorage by 8:00 the following morning. We'd be flying out in an iconic De Havilland Beaver, a big floatplane designed especially for bush flying. It was famous as a workhorse in backcountry flying throughout Canada and Alaska. The trip from Ely, across the border into Lac la Croix was about 35 miles by floatplane and would only take about 20 minutes.

Before leaving the outfitter, I bought a new map specific to the area we'd be exploring. We all four now had the same map, a 1:50,000 scale topographic map, centered on Poohbah Lake that covered the entire area we'd be exploring. After discussing our planned route with one of the guys at the outfitter, he made several marks on one of them, showing an excellent campsite on Conmee and an unnamed lake just east of it and north of Suzanette Lake that had some terrific fishing, being more or less landlocked, and receiving almost no fishing pressure. He also made notations showing landmarks and several of the portages we'd likely encounter on the path that had been chosen for this year's trek.

Tom also bought his paddle, which had a thin, slightly curved blade that was flat across the end. I could see how it could be easily damaged or broken if not handled properly. He paid a pretty penny for it, and I assumed it was worth the money.

Once we had everything squared away with the outfitter, we headed out in search of some dinner. We were all starved. I hadn't had anything to eat since breakfast earlier that morning with Mary Jane and the kids. That now seemed like ages ago, though it had only been a little less than twelve hours.

There was nothing fancy about Ely or its choice of restaurants. We chose a place that just seemed to fit, built of logs with a knotty pine interior and booths lining the walls. The place was bustling with guys mostly like us, coming and going. Finding an empty booth, a waitress appeared with water and menus. After a brief review of the choices, we all ordered burgers, fries, and soft drinks. While we waited for our food, we went over our list for the grocery store which was to be our last stop before heading back to the motel.

After dinner, we all pitched in ten bucks and headed out to buy fresh supplies from our list. The local grocery catered to campers and stayed open late during the busy tourist season. We bought three dozen eggs, three pounds of bacon, a small country ham, a five pound sack of potatoes, several packages of Oreo cookies, spaghetti, butter, pure maple syrup, pancake mix, flour, a couple of loaves of bread, instant coffee, sugar, salt, and a couple of big jars of peanut butter. Forty bucks went a pretty long way in 1981.

As the cashier rang us up, I wondered to myself how we were going to pack and carry all this stuff. I had faith that these guys had done this many times before, so I just went with the flow. Grocery sacks in hand, we got in the car and headed back to the motel to begin our final preparations for tomorrow... trying to stuff everything we had into these six backpacks.

We had two rooms but decided to bring everything into one to do the sorting and packing together. We'd bought a six-pack of cold beer when we got our supplies, so this would be our last opportunity to imbibe until we returned. We were not bringing any alcohol into the park. The water in Quetico was pure and crystal clear, and that would be our only source of liquid for the next eight days.

The first thing we did was pack our own individual backpacks. We'd all brought a similar assortment of personal items and found that they all fit easily into our packs with a little room to spare. It was a good thing too, as we began to fill the two remaining packs with food, cooking utensils, tent poles, ropes, camp stove, a small propane bottle and the rest of the little odds and ends we would need.

With the two common packs stuffed, we had some leftover food that we split up amongst our own personal packs. Since we would be consuming the perishable foods early on, the loads would lighten a little each day, but to start, these packs were bursting at the seams. The two common packs were the heaviest. We didn't have any means to weigh them, but we guessed they were somewhere in the 35 to 40-pound range. They would feel every bit of that on our first few portages, but at least we'd found a place for everything.

With everything packed up and neatly stacked next to the door, we finished the last two beers, and Tom and I went to our room to try and get some sleep. We'd all had a long day of travel and were tired. Since we had to be at the seaplane anchorage by 8:00, we agreed to check out early enough to have a quick breakfast at the same place we'd eaten dinner, before heading to the seaplane anchorage in the morning.

Going to our room, we each decided to take a hot shower before turning in. It would be our last opportunity for the next eight days.

The last thing I remember from this day was reaching to turn out the light.

Day 1

It seemed like my head had just hit the pillow when the motel's clock radio went off with an annoying *bzzz...bzzz...bzzz*. Tom and I were both fumbling for the off button. He found it first and our feet hit the floor simultaneously as I tried to orient myself to where the hell I was. When I finally realized consciousness, I got excited for the day to begin. I'd been looking forward to this specific morning for nearly three months and it was finally here.

Having showered the night before, all we had to do was brush our teeth, check out and pack the car. Wayne and Bill were already loading their gear when Tom and I opened our door. We grabbed our stuff and joined in, stuffing packs wherever we could for the short ride ahead. Checking out of the motel, we headed for breakfast, which would be our last meal in civilization for the next eight days. We had toast, hash browns, eggs, and sausage since we'd be having plenty of bacon for the next few days.

After paying our bills, we hopped in the car and headed for the seaplane anchorage. It was a gorgeous morning, cool but sunny and dead calm, the dew glistening in the trees. Upon arriving, there was a beautiful, blue and white DeHavilland Beaver tied to the dock where the pilot was talking to a dock hand.

Being a bit of an airplane nut, I have flown in many different types of small planes and even came within a whisker of getting my private pilot's license before the cost of maintaining it hit me, but I'd never had a ride in a DeHavilland Beaver. We carried the first load to the dock and introduced ourselves. The pilot (fittingly named "Dusty" Miller), and the dock hand, started loading our gear into the baggage compartment while Tom and I went back to the car for the last of it. After locking the car, we carried the last two packs, along with our fishing rods, to the dock. All the rods were broken down and tied together with rubber bands, so everything fit into the baggage compartment except for Tom's new paddle. Unphased, Dusty tied it to the float struts and it was time to climb aboard.

Wayne got into the right front seat next to Dusty, while Tom, Bill and I squeezed ourselves into the cramped rear seat. After making sure we were all properly buckled up and the doors were latched, he asked if we were ready to go. Our enthusiastic response affirmed that we were, and he asked the dock hand to untie us and push us off. Yelling "clear" out his small window, Dusty pushed the primer a few times and hit the starter. The prop began to turn, and the big Pratt & Whitney radial engine sputtered a few times, then caught and roared to life amidst a puff of white smoke from the exhaust.

He adjusted the fuel mixture and throttle and the engine settled into a steady, rumbling idle. As we slowly taxied away from the dock, he set the flaps and propeller pitch for takeoff. It being a dead calm morning, there was no need to line up into the wind to takeoff. All there was ahead of us was beautiful, clear, blue water. I looked at my watch. It was exactly 8:20.

Once we'd cleared the dock sufficiently, so that the prop wash wouldn't cause a windstorm on shore, Dusty checked to be sure the path ahead was clear. Giving the engine instruments one last look, he pushed the throttle all the way forward and we gathered speed, coming up "on plane" like a speeding boat. The lake's surface was smooth as glass, and the surface tension didn't want to let go of the floats. As we gained a little more speed, Dusty gave the yoke a gentle "push-pull" to break the water's hold and suddenly we were airborne and climbing.

Cruising due north at about 800 feet, the water wonderland below was a sight to behold in the golden early morning light. There was nothing but water and tree-covered islands as far as the eye could see. Giant boulders and rocky outcroppings gave testament to the glaciers that covered this land some 10,000 years ago. When the glaciers melted and receded, this is what they left behind. It seemed such a maze, I wondered how we would be able to navigate it without getting totally lost. I also wondered how Dusty knew where the hell he was going. Everything looked the same to my untrained eye. It was a bewildering patchwork of water and islands with no discernable landmarks.

About 20 minutes later, he began a slow left turn, reduced power, and lined up for an approach to a lake that to me, looked no different than all the rest. I couldn't see a ranger station or any other sign of habitation. Dusty lowered the flaps to slow our descent, adjusted prop pitch again, and when we gently touched the water, I could see the spray coming off the floats glistening in the morning sunlight. Slowing quickly, we turned left to taxi towards the tree covered shore. Finally, I saw a small, white building that turned out to be the ranger station and a dock extending about fifty feet out into the lake. To the left of the dock was a small beach with about a half dozen aluminum canoes neatly lining the shore, turned upside down so as not to fill with water when it rained.

Dusty deftly maneuvered the plane and cut the engine, perfectly timed to coast gently into the dock so the left float touched with barely a bump. I admired his skills and told him so. I could tell he appreciated the compliment as he said he'd been bush-flying for over 30 years, twelve of them in Alaska where he'd really honed his skills.

With a practiced grace, he effortlessly hopped down onto the left float and tied us down. While we disembarked, trying not to trip over the struts, a ranger came walking down the dock to greet us. We followed him to the white building so he could check us in while Dusty emptied the baggage compartment and stacked our gear in a neat pile on the dock.

The ranger cleared us through customs using just our American driver's licenses for ID. We showed him our park reservations and fishing licenses and he issued us our camping permits. We then signed for our canoes and confirmed with him that it was our intent to return on August 9th. He said the return floatplane would be here right around 3:00pm, so we needed to plan accordingly.

He handed us each a paddle (Tom was right, they were very stout) and we headed over to find our canoes. We turned them right side up and pushed them into the water to check for any leaks. Finding none, we pulled them part way back onto the narrow beach and went to the dock to retrieve our gear. We all shook hands with Dusty, thanking him for a beautiful flight and said we hoped he was the pilot assigned to pick us up in eight days. After carrying our gear to the canoes, we began finding the most efficient way to fit everything in while leaving room to sit and maneuver.

Having loaded the canoes with all our gear, which we'd carefully distributed to balance the weight, we finally pushed off around 9:30am with the warm August sun at our backs, glinting off the calm waters of Lac la Croix. I was ecstatic as the adventure had finally begun. I'd been dreaming of and preparing for this moment ever since Tom called me back in early May. As a canoeing novice, I was relegated to the bow of the craft where my primary, and most important job, was to stay centered so as not to upset the delicate balance and dump all our gear into the deep clear waters of Lac La Croix.

My secondary duty was to help provide propulsion by paddling. It was an awkward start as I splashed and banged my paddle against the aluminum gunwale while trying to push water to the rear, thereby propelling the canoe forward. Tom was in the stern with his new paddle, simultaneously propelling and steering the craft with every efficient stroke. He offered no criticism, but also no advice. He let me work it out for myself, and I silently thanked him for that.

It didn't take me long to get the hang of it as I carefully observed Bill and Wayne slightly ahead and to our right leading the way across the glassy surface. I watched as Bill, in the bow, made long quiet strokes where he silently dipped the paddle and pulled. I also noticed Wayne in the stern making similarly quiet strokes, at the end of which he would hold the paddle briefly as a rudder to offset slight turns resulting from his bow-mate's stroke, whether on the port or starboard side of the canoe.

I was a keen observer of the mechanics and within the first hour, I was mimicking their technique. I was so caught up in the act of canoeing that I had failed to notice that we were no longer anywhere near the ranger station where we had begun. Nor was there any sign of habitation anywhere I looked. I began to really see the wild beauty all around us; blue water, blue skies, wild shorelines near and far, islands big and small covered with pines, cedars and spruce, huge granite boulders, and puffy white fair-weather clouds floating overhead. There were no motorboats, water skiers, canoes, airplanes... nothing to detract from the sheer natural beauty of this watery wonderland. Also noticeable was the lack of man-made debris of any kind. We'd heard somewhere that the motto of Quetico Provincial Park is to leave nothing behind but your footprints. Whether official or not, it would be our guide this week. I was really enjoying myself and couldn't keep the smile off my face.

As we made our way, silently gliding around islands, we traced our progress on our topo maps. The night before, we had marked the intended route on all the maps so that we could look for landmarks. The plan was to head through Brewer and McAree Lakes to Pond Lake then portage to Gratton Lake. From there we would move on to Wicksteed, Darky, William and finally Conmee where we would spend a couple of days. Our return would be southwest into Brent, back into Darky, then through the Darky River into Minn Lake and back into Lac la Croix, thereby completing a rough figure eight pattern. It was an ambitious trip for eight days and it would be very easy to get hopelessly lost here if you didn't pay close attention. We had an open map in each canoe, and if there was any disagreement on a given landmark, we would stop and double check until we were all certain of our location. There would be no help unless we chanced upon another canoeist who knew where they were. That being a very unlikely scenario, we all paid close attention to our navigation.

About three hours into the trip we approached our first portage. Not long after we'd entered a short, nameless river, we could hear a rapids up ahead and pulled the canoes ashore to scout the best way around them. Finding a well-worn path around the rapids, we decided to stop and take a lunch break. Since we hadn't yet done any fishing, we obviously had no fish for a shore lunch, so we broke out the bread and peanut butter for a brief bit of mid-day nourishment. We quenched our thirst by simply dipping a tin cup in the river. It was important that we not dawdle too much as the plan was to try to get to somewhere on or near Wicksteed Lake by tonight.

Our first portage was a short one, only about 300 yards or so, but it gave me a taste of what lay ahead. Bill and Wayne were good-sized guys and they each flipped a canoe over their heads, balanced the yoke on their shoulders and started down the path looking like a couple of big turtles. Tom and I shouldered the two heaviest packs, filled with food and cooking gear, and followed. About ten minutes later, arriving below the rapids, we deposited our loads, then headed back for the remaining packs plus our fishing rods. On the way back we stopped briefly to admire the natural beauty of the swiftly running water. It was mesmerizing, much like watching the gentle flames and orange glow of a campfire. Even today, I find a special peace and solace in these two things, helping me put my problems aside for the night and drift off to sleep.

By the time we paddled away from shore, we'd spent about an hour and were feeling a little tired in the shoulders from the continuous paddling but otherwise, refreshed by the nourishment.

Traversing the northern part of McAree Lake, we decided to break out the fishing gear and troll as we paddled. Tom said it was a pretty effective way to fish, and it was fun to just get a line in the water and see what happened. Apparently, they'd caught a lot of fish this way simply by accident.

Slowly drifting in a gentle breeze, we each set up one rod and reel. We were all using only spinning gear. We each had our favorite lures like Rapalas, River Runts, spoons, and plugs of one kind or another. Wayne tied on a red and white Daredevil, famous for catching big northern pike. We cast out and took up our paddles once again, a line running on each side of our canoes. I found I had to adjust my paddling a bit so as not to catch my own line. These were mostly deep waters, so snags were of little concern.

As we made our way through McAree Lake, I began to think about French explorers who'd lived here and trapped these waters a few hundred years ago, supplying beaver pelts to their European homelands. We were probably seeing this watery country in the same way they saw it... from canoes. The winters here would be brutal. The lakes would freeze solid, probably with as much as a foot or two of ice, topped with as much, or more, of snow. Navigating this country in the dead of winter would be on foot or snowshoes, but what of the transition periods? Fall and spring would be difficult when ice would not be safe, making lake travel impossible.

I then wondered to myself when this area had first seen human habitation. Was it before or after the last great ice age? What did this land look like before the glaciers began slowly, imperceptibly, plowing through the rock? I became mesmerized watching my paddle dipping silently and creating beautiful little whirlpools as I pulled the blade through the cold clear water. Being in a quiet, beautiful, wild setting like this was proving to be hypnotic.

Thunk! My fishing rod was nearly pulled out of the canoe. I quickly grabbed it before it went overboard while laying my paddle across the gunwale. "Fish on!" I exclaimed. Everyone stopped paddling and reeled in their lines to avoid getting tangled. About twenty feet from the boat a smallmouth bass jumped and landed with a splash, the line tightening again and zinging to my left then to my right. "Smallies" are well-known for their scrappiness and ability to jump clear of the water, and this one put on quite a show. After a brief 2-3-minute struggle I got it next to the canoe and lip-landed it. I estimated it to be maybe three pounds, not a monster, but a beautiful fish with deep bronze-colored markings. I unhooked and gently released it, watching as it swam under the canoe and disappeared, likely wondering what the hell just happened.

After that, we all just drifted for a few minutes, chatting about the beauty of the place before discussing how far we should go on this first day. We pulled beside each other and compared our maps, just to be sure we all agreed exactly where we were. Our trip would eventually take us into Darky Lake where there are some very old, native pictographs on sheer rock walls. Tom and the guys had been to Darky on past trips, but had always approached it from the south, so this was new territory for them as well as for me.

We decided to press on through the northern part of McAree Lake, then into Pond Lake where we would face one of the longest portages of the whole trip. We agreed that getting through this portage on the first day would put us within striking distance of Wicksteed. We wanted to be sure we still had ample daylight to scout a camp site and set up for the night.

Traversing the narrows between McAree and Pond Lakes was gorgeous. As we rounded a bend and the view widened into Pond Lake, Tom pointed ahead to a small island with several tall trees and said "eagle!" This was the first of several bald eagle sightings we were fortunate to enjoy on this trip. The sun shone on its unmistakable white head as it perched majestically on a tall branch surveying its domain. We all stopped paddling and reached for our cameras. In 1981, bald eagles were an endangered species, and this was one of the early highlights of our journey. As we found out much later, our photographs didn't come close to doing justice to what we'd seen and felt at that moment.

The water remained calm as we paddled silently through the reflections toward the northeast corner of Pond Lake to what we hoped was a well-marked portage. As we approached the shore, everything looked the same. We turned left for several hundred yards and couldn't pick out anything resembling a trail, then reversed and went back the other way, scrutinizing every foot of shoreline looking for any sign of traffic. We went even closer to shore, now only about twenty feet away and went back again. Little daggers of doubt began to nag at our consciousness. Were we in the right place... were we lost?

Finally, Wayne pointed to a small space beside a couple of boulders that looked like it may offer some promise. We pulled ashore and got out to stretch our legs. There was a narrow opening in the weeds that looked like it may be a path. Wayne scouted ahead and found a definite pathway that was overgrown with grasses but appeared to be navigable on foot. He went on for a couple hundred feet and confirmed that this appeared to be the portage we were looking for.

We emptied the canoes and put our cameras safely back in the packs. This time, Tom and Wayne hefted the canoes and started off into what to me seemed like oblivion. Bill and I dutifully followed with the heaviest packs. Yelling ahead, we told them to slow down and let us pass so we could lead the way because we had better visibility, both front and sideways. We were on the lookout for bears.

The path wandered through a grassy area, then up into the woods before dropping down to a boggy, wet, swampy area where the footing was slick and sloppy. We turned and warned the canoe haulers behind us of what lay ahead. On we went for another 15 minutes or so with no end in sight. Downed trees crossed the path. This portage was a nightmare! After gaining some higher ground, we found a small clearing and stopped to rest while waiting for Tom and Wayne to catch up. They were a hundred yards or so behind us. When they arrived, they dumped the canoes and we all sat for about ten minutes to catch our breath while pondering how much further we had to go. We'd been hiking for about 20 minutes and estimated we'd gone less than a half mile. We also hoped we were on the right portage and would come out on the west end of what the map indicated should be Gratton Lake. If we were right, it would only be about another mile or two of paddling to get in to Wicksteed.

At this point, we switched tasks letting Tom and Bill shoulder the packs and lead the way, while Wayne and I hefted the canoes. This was my first attempt at carrying a canoe on my back and it didn't go well. As I lifted it over my head, I was suddenly top-heavy and clumsily stumbled left, then right, then awkwardly down in a heap with my feet in the air and the canoe up against a tree. This brought roars of laughter from my "buddies". The only thing hurt was my pride and their laughter was so infectious that we all sat there in hysterics until we got it out of our systems and could go on. This time, Tom helped me get the beast balanced so I could stay on my feet. Once I got going, I was okay, but it was heavier than I imagined. I guess I wasn't in the shape I thought I was!

Stumbling forward, I was hoping to hell we'd find the end soon. It took another fifteen grueling minutes, but I heard Tom yell back to us that he'd reached Gratton Lake. Music to my ears! I was dying of thirst and when I reached the end and deposited my canoe, Tom handed me his tin cup and I dipped it into Gratton Lake and poured three cupfuls down my throat as fast as I could swallow. Drenched in sweat, we contemplated a swim right then and there. Instead, we rifled through one of the packs for the Oreo cookies and took a cookie break before heading back for the rest of our gear.

The trip back seemed much shorter without carrying a load, but this portage had to be more than a half mile, maybe as long as three quarters of a mile. That doesn't seem like much unless you're carrying 40 pounds through bogs and woods and over downed timber. I fervently hoped that this would be the worst of the portages. Arriving back where we'd started, we each grabbed a backpack along with our fishing rods and began the trek back to Gratton, where we once again loaded our gear into the canoes and paddled away towards Wicksteed.

There was another narrows of about a mile that caused us to check our maps again. We all agreed, if we didn't come out onto bigger water after about 20 minutes of paddling, we would have to reassess our navigation.

About fifteen minutes later, we could see a wider expanse in the distance and we silently took a deep breath. We had finally arrived at the western tip of Wicksteed Lake, our intended destination for day one. As we entered the lake it was coming up on 6:00pm, giving us nearly three hours before sunset to find a campsite, set up the tent and make some dinner.

Wicksteed was a big lake dotted with islands of all sizes. We paddled past several before finding one that looked perfect for our first night in Quetico. It was rather small and should be free of bears unless one decided to swim out to greet us. It had an easy access point so we could pull the canoes up onto dry land to unload. We found it already had a fire pit circled in rocks with a flat area about 10 feet above the water line that would be perfect for pitching the tent. It also had a huge, smooth, granite boulder to sit on and watch the sun go down over the water.

We all pitched in getting the packs out. Tom and I began setting up the tent while Wayne & Bill got out the camp stove and cooking gear. We were all hungry and tired from a long day of paddling and portaging. There was some discussion about trying to catch a fish for dinner, but all agreed we didn't want to wait, so it would be fried potatoes, ham, and eggs. Wayne fired up the propane camp stove and put on the frying pan. He put in a pat of butter and sliced some ham to fry while I peeled and sliced a couple of potatoes. When the ham started to crisp a little around the edges, he started cracking eggs...it all smelled wonderful! The tin plates and utensils came from the outfitter along with the packs and as the eggs came off the pan and onto our plates, he put on more. We sat on logs and all enjoyed our first real meal since breakfast that morning in Ely.

After dinner, we took off our shoes and socks, emptied our pockets and jumped into the lake to rid ourselves of the day's sweat and grime. The shock of the cold water took my breath away, but a few seconds later felt invigorating. We dog paddled, slapped water at each other and generally had a great time for a few minutes. We swam to shore and stepped out to grab our towels. Stripping off the clothes of the day, we wrung them out by hand and considered them "washed". We dried off and got into clean, fresh clothes and put up a clothesline rope to dry our clean ones.

What a day it had been. The sun was getting low in the western sky and the evening light was perfect. We started a small campfire for the ambiance of it and to heat some water for hot chocolate. We took our cups out on the boulder and just soaked up the peace and quiet of the place. There was a contrail in the sky heading from northwest to southeast. It was so high we couldn't hear it, but I marveled at that aluminum tube some five miles overhead probably going 500 miles per hour with a hundred or more people in it who were oblivious to the beauty we were enjoying directly below them. I wondered where they were coming from, and where they were going. Wherever it was, I doubt it could hold a candle to Quetico.

As the sun finally dipped below the trees on the far shore, we could hardly keep our eyes open. It had been a terrific first day in the wilderness, and one I'd never forget.

Day 2

I had wondered the night before if it would be awkward sleeping four guys in one tent, side-by-side like sardines in a can. At home, I was in the habit of reading in bed until I got sleepy, but we were all so tired from the fresh air and exercise that I barely remembered even getting into the tent. The sleep had been instant, deep, and refreshing.

We began to stir just as the dawn was breaking. Exiting the tent one by one, as we surveyed our surroundings, the air was fresh and cool and a wisp of fog on lay on the surface of the lake. Finding my pack, I dug out a sweatshirt to ward off the early morning chill. It looked like it would be another beautiful day with barely a cloud in the sky. I roamed around the small island picking up deadwood for a fire to heat some water for coffee. I estimated the island to be no more than about 300 yards long by maybe 150 yards wide. Being an avid golfer, I was pretty good at estimating distances by yards.

After dumping an armful of firewood next to the pit, I set about starting a fire using pinecones and twigs for kindling. Soon, I had a small fire going and balanced the coffee pot on some rocks. We were cheating a little by using instant coffee, but it was satisfying, nonetheless.

Having no pressing agenda for the day, we spread out our maps and discussed what we wanted to do. Since the ultimate goal for the day was to reach Conmee Lake, we would head in that direction but with less urgency than we'd felt yesterday to make progress. There were some very promising areas to fish on the way. During previous trips, Bill said they had caught a lot of fish in the area where the Darky River flowed out of Darky Lake, so that's where we were first headed today.

We enjoyed a hearty breakfast of bacon and pancakes, courtesy of Bill, the designated cook for the day. Afterward, we all pitched in to clean up the dishes, break down the tent, retrieve our still damp clothes from the rope line, properly douse the fire and check the campsite to be sure we left nothing behind but the wet ashes of our campfire. The sun was getting higher in the sky and burning off the early morning fog and the water was as still as glass as we packed up the canoes and paddled away to the east. I asked Tom if the lakes were usually this calm. He laughed derisively and said, "trust me, we will have wind before this trip is over!"

It only took about an hour to reach Darky Lake. Keeping a keen eye out for wildlife, we saw a pair of loons, a muskrat, geese, and ducks. We also saw a couple of small mammals swimming but couldn't get close enough to properly identify them. My guess was either mink or otters. At one point we saw a couple of deer that had come to the lake to drink, a doe and a fawn I presumed from their sizes.

Once again, I was struck by the lack of any sign of human activity. The place was desolate, beautiful, and spiritual. I loved looking for the little things tucked in amongst the overall majesty of Quetico. I particularly noticed how the gnarled, exposed roots of ancient cedars clung to their rocky anchors. I loved seeing turtles sunning themselves on logs extending into the water, birds flitting about the trees, chipmunks scurrying about fallen pinecones, and how the sun sparkled off the gentle wake of Wayne and Bill's canoe. It felt like we were intruding on the lives of the creatures that called Quetico home.

I snapped out of my reverie as we came upon a small stream flowing into the lake and set up our rods to begin some serious fishing. Drifting about fifty yards out from where the stream spilled into the lake, before I could even get a line in the water Wayne had a fish on. Tom and I watched as Wayne played the fish, rod tip dipping as the fish dove deep. It wasn't jumping so I guessed it was either a walleye, or a northern pike rather than a smallmouth. A few minutes later, Bill scooped the fish up in the net, and after some fumbling around in the bottom of the canoe, Wayne held up a nice walleye. Although we planned on having a shore lunch today of pan-fried walleye, Wayne decided to throw this one back since it was still early and we'd, no doubt, catch plenty more fish before lunchtime.

Over the next couple of hours, we caught and released at least two dozen more fish, mostly walleyes and smallmouth bass, but also a couple of nice pike, one of which was about three feet long. That translates to about ten pounds. Pike are very bony and hard to fillet so we didn't keep any, but they were a lot of fun to catch. Besides, why would anyone want to eat a pike when you have plenty of walleye, or trout on-hand?

As the sun rose overhead, it was now time to keep a couple of fish for lunch. Walleye in the two-pound range are perfect for eating. Of course, the fish decided not to cooperate as if they knew it was nearing mealtime. We cast, we trolled, and we changed lures. It seemed like the fish had just left the area. We were a little perplexed and finally decided to move on, heading about a quarter mile further east to where we found a rocky point extending into the lake.

Bingo! Fish on, then another. In the span of about five minutes we had two nice walleyes in the 2-3-pound range. We paddled on, looking for a good spot to pull ashore where there was room for the canoes and a place to set up the camp stove and soon found a spot that also had a bonus feature of a downed tree to sit on while we ate.

After pulling the canoes up on a narrow beach, we got out the cooking gear. Using my paddle as a cutting board, I prepared four nice fillets. Herring Gulls appeared from out of nowhere to feast on the walleye innards and leftovers that I threw out into the lake. Nothing was wasted in Quetico.

Bill got out the flour, mixed in a little salt and pepper, then dusted the fillets while the butter was melting in the frying pan. Tom cut up a potato into thin slices and in short order, we had a classic shore lunch. If you've ever enjoyed fresh-caught walleye in the wilderness, you understand what I mean. If not, no amount of description could do it justice. Everything just tasted better outdoors.

After eating, we just relaxed and soaked up the fresh air and sunshine for a while, chatting about this and that, feeling grateful for where we were and the superb weather we were enjoying. Eventually, the maps were brought out and we discussed our plans for the rest of the day. I asked if we were going to see the pictographs they'd told me about here in Darky Lake. Tom said they were in the south end of Darky Lake, a couple of miles away, closer to where we'd be entering on our return trip out of Brent on Thursday, so we'd see them then. Today, there were two more long portages ahead before we'd reach Conmee Lake. On the maps, they seemed nearly as long as the Gratton portage we did yesterday, which was a little unsettling.

The first was only about a half hour away and it would take us into a couple of nameless lakes before coming out into William Lake. Depending on our progress, we might make Conmee by evening. If not, we could find a campsite in William Lake and then arrive in Conmee before noon tomorrow. None of us were looking forward to two long portages on the same day, but we'd had a good night's sleep and a good meal, so we just decided to see how we felt later in the day. Once we left Darky Lake, this would be new territory to us all.

Cleaning our dishes, we made sure we'd left nothing behind and loaded the cooking packs back into the canoes. Tom asked if I'd like to try the stern for a while. I said "Sure, I've been paying attention, gimme a shot." I hopped into the stern seat while Tom pushed us off and jumped into the bow. We got the craft turned in the right direction and Tom said "Here, you can try my new paddle." After swapping, we headed northeast towards the small, nameless lake that would lead to the first of the two major portages we faced.

Having watched Wayne and Bill for a day and a half now, I got the hang of steering a canoe in pretty short order. Tom's paddle really did feel different; it was much lighter and easier to handle. I told Tom, "This is like a Porsche paddle... mine is like a pickup truck paddle." Chuckling, he agreed. Steering with it was a breeze as we headed into a short choke point that then opened into a small, nameless lake. We went straight across, hoping that this portage trailhead would be much easier to find than the one we almost missed yesterday. With very little breeze again today, it was starting to get hot.

As we approached the northeast shoreline, we picked up a light spot in the trees that we hoped was our trailhead. The closer we got, the more confident we became. Pulling ashore, we saw that there was a well-defined path that had obviously seen a lot of use over the years. I began to wonder, was this a path used by the natives of this area hundreds, even thousands of years ago? Maybe so. It was humbling to think that we might be walking the same path that explorers had been using for centuries. It also boosted our confidence to realize we were exactly where we thought we were.

This time, Tom and I led the way with the packs while Wayne and Bill hefted the canoes. The path started in an open grassy section but soon after, entered a dark wooded area with exposed roots of gnarly old cedars. About ten minutes later, we broke out into a meadow and found wild blueberries lining a portion of the path.

The berries were much smaller than what you would buy in a grocery store but were just as tasty. It also reminded us to be "bear aware" and we began yelling out "Hey Bear!" It was past cub birthing season, so the spring cubs would be pretty hefty by now but also still attached at the hip to mama bear. Seeing some bear scat, we knew they'd been in the area. Wayne and Bill heard us calling out "hey bear" and started doing the same. The last thing in the world we wanted to do was to surprise a mama bear and her half-grown cubs!

With the path so well-defined, this portage was easier than our nightmare portage of the day before, though it was very hot, and we all stopped to rest for a few minutes in the shade of the next wooded section. Since we didn't carry any water with us, we would have nothing to drink until we reached the other end. Even though Tom and I offered to tote the canoes the rest of the way, Bill and Wayne insisted on toughing it out and after another ten minutes or so, we saw water ahead. After dropping off our loads, we found our tin cups and drank like we'd never be satisfied.

This end of the portage opened into a narrows rather than a big lake. Resting for a few minutes before heading back for the remainder of our gear, we also wisely, thought to bring our cups back with us so we could have another drink at the other end. We headed back the way we'd come, talking loudly and yelling "hey bear" every so often. Walking straight back without a load only took us about twenty minutes so we estimated this portage to be about a third of a mile, but easier than yesterday's because it was wider and better defined. After another drink and a five-minute breather, we strapped on the last four packs and picked up our fishing rods. Upon returning to the other end again, we figured we'd spent about an hour on this portage. It was now about 2:30 and Tom invited me to stay in the stern, though he wanted his paddle back.

Leaving this portage behind and paddling away, we headed through the narrows which was maybe 200 yards wide and lined with huge pines, cedars, spruce, and boulder outcroppings. Steering with the commercial paddle was no problem, though it was noticeably heavier.

About twenty minutes and a few gentle bends later, we saw ahead of us an opening to a medium-sized unnamed lake. When we got into the main portion of the lake, we pulled beside each other for another navigation check. We all agreed that we needed to hug the right shoreline which should take us into yet another narrows before entering another small lake.

After our map check, we decided to fish this section, and breaking out our fishing rods, we began to troll again. The scenery was spectacular as we quietly paddled our way past small islands with scraggly trees that could, no doubt, tell some harrowing tales of wind and weather.

Suddenly, Bill shouted, "fish on!" and we all reeled in our lines to watch. Judging from the way his rod was bent double, this was a *very* big fish. It kept fighting deep, pulling Bill's rod tip down into the water, while we all speculated on its size and what it was. This fish wasn't giving and inch; we could hear Bill's drag clicking as the fish kept diving for the bottom away from shore, pulling their canoe along with it. Tom said it was probably a lake trout, adding that they'd caught some pretty big ones in years past.

This battle had been going strong for fifteen minutes and we still hadn't caught a glimpse of the fish. We could tell the fish was tiring as Bill was finally gaining some line, lifting his rod then reeling again until the rod tip touched the water, then lifting once more. A couple of minutes later he had a beautiful lake trout beside the canoe. Wayne netted the fish and Bill unhooked it, holding it up for pictures. He estimated it was at least fifteen pounds and matched anything they'd caught in the eight years they'd been doing these trips. We were only a few feet from their canoe when Bill gently released this beautiful fish. Weary from the fight, it wallowed close to the surface for about 30 seconds regaining its strength, then slowly swam away into the depths of this big unnamed puddle in the middle of nowhere. We sat quietly, enjoying a few long moments of appreciation before taking up our paddles to move on.

Casting out our lines once again, we trolled the southern shoreline as we made our way eastward towards the narrows. Keeping the lines in the water through the narrows and into the next smaller lake, we had no further activity. Once we cleared the narrows into the main part of the lake, we determined from the maps that we should go straight through, heading due south then east through another narrows, which would take us into the western end of William Lake. Upon arriving in William, we would have about two or three miles to the northeastern end and the final portage into Conmee. The maps showed this portage to be a straight line, west to east and we estimated it to be at least a half mile, maybe a bit more. We hoped it wouldn't be the beast that we'd had yesterday going into Gratton!

It was now mid-afternoon, and I guessed it would take an hour or so of steady paddling to reach the Conmee portage. Barring any unpleasant surprises, we should be able to set up camp at our destination tonight. It was our intent to spend three nights in Conmee and take a day trip from our base camp into the unnamed lake recommended by our outfitter back in Ely, then spend one more day exploring Conmee itself.

We paddled steadily, though not hurriedly, across William Lake from west to east, and trolling all the while, we picked up a couple of smaller fish, one walleye and one small northern but released them both. Along the way, we passed several good-looking campsites, all of which were unoccupied. There had been no sign of humanity since leaving the ranger station, and we felt very fortunate having these beautiful lakes to ourselves.

As we approached the northeastern tip of William, it began to get shallow with lots of smaller rocks, bowling ball sized boulders, lily pads, wild rice and grasses. The portage had to be here somewhere, and that "somewhere" turned out to be on the other side of this small boulder field. Wading into the water, we dragged the canoes most of the way to the shoreline, but then had to unload the canoes and carry everything about 50 yards or so over these slippery rocks, to semi-dry land where the boggy portage began. Once we'd deposited all the packs, we had to wade back out and carry the canoes ashore. The small, round boulders made for a very tough go of it, so we each grabbed an end, half-carrying and half-dragging them the last 50 yards.

This portage was muddy, wet, and sloppy, but thankfully, not as long as we'd feared. It was maybe a third of a mile and loaded with mosquitoes. This was the first time we'd been bothered much by mosquitoes, and I wondered if it was the shallow water that provided a perfect breeding ground for them. Before setting out, we dug through the packs for the bug juice we'd forgotten about and gave ourselves a good coating. This was a tough portage, not for the length, but for the clouds of mosquitoes and the muddy, sloppy conditions combined with the heat and lack of any breeze.

Finally reaching the Conmee side, we found ourselves in a bay of sorts and had to head south, then east to reach the main lake. Still, we'd made it all the way to Conmee in two days of fairly easy paddling. Conmee was loaded with islands but we headed straight for the medium sized island in the southern part (towards

Suzanette Lake) that our outfitter had marked as a good site. After about 20 minutes, we paddled up to the marked island about 6:00. It was indeed perfect, and thankfully, unoccupied, as were all the other sites we passed. It appeared that we had Conmee all to ourselves!

The campsite was everything our outfitter said it would be. It had a narrow beach, huge, smooth boulder outcroppings, and a gently sloping rise to a large, flat area with a nice sized fire pit and plenty of room for the tent. Someone had even made a crude, but surprisingly comfortable, "easy chair" out of slate-like flat rocks that sat near the top of the slope facing the water to the south. We all had to try it out, snapping pictures and generally praising the brilliance of its design. The ten to fifteen-foot elevation above the water made for a wonderful perspective, like sitting on a balcony. The enormous granite outcropping was slightly rounded and provided another spectacular view to the east.

With a couple of hours of daylight left, we unloaded all our gear, set up the tent, then grabbed our fishing rods, and walked down to the waterline to explore our private island and see if we could snag a couple of walleyes for dinner. The lake was so calm, Tom and I decided to hop in our canoe and slowly paddle clockwise around the island, casting for fish, while

Wayne and Bill walked out on the eastern point where some rocks offered some solid footing and allowed them to cast in a wide arc.

I boated a small walleye, maybe a pound, but released it to allow it to grow up. Tom caught a small northern, sometimes referred to as a "hammer-handle" because it was skinny and only about 18" long. When we came around the back side of the island, we still hadn't caught our dinner, though when we reached the eastern tip, Wayne and Bill had two nice walleyes and were already walking the shoreline back to where we'd beached the canoes. Tom and I followed and pulled our canoe up next to the other. I filleted the two fish while the others got out the cooking gear and began to prepare potatoes and a pot of spaghetti. It sounds funny now, but spaghetti, walleye and fried potatoes are wonderful together, especially on an island in the wilds of Canada after a long, hot day of paddling and portaging.

Having finished dinner, we cleaned up our mess, emptied our pockets and took a running leap into the lake. As it was the night before, the water was shockingly cold at first, but words cannot describe how refreshing this was after another really hot day. After swimming, diving, and dog paddling, we again rigged a clothesline and hung our wet, but now clean, clothes to dry.

Since this was a bigger island and close to the lake's eastern shore, maybe only a hundred yards or so away, we decided to take bear precautions with our food stores. We rigged another line between two trees and hung the food packs about 15 feet off the ground and about the same distance from each tree. Since we'd be here for three nights and two days, we debated whether to take all the food with us during our day trips. No sense in tempting fate (and bears) while we were away from base.

As the sun was setting, it appeared we'd have another beautiful, clear night. We heated water for hot chocolate, then took our air mattresses out to the boulders and sat. We chatted awhile, reliving the day, and when it got dark, we lay back and stared up at the most impressive night sky I'd ever seen. Having never been anywhere so void of light pollution, I found the sky absolutely stunning. None of us knew much about astronomy, but we could pick out the big and little dippers, as well as Polaris, the north star.

We also saw several light specks moving steadily across the sky. Bill said these were satellites... we counted five of them that night and they all looked like tiny, moving stars. It made us all feel so small, sitting on a rock looking at billions of stars like our own, many of which may not even exist today.

Imagine if each of those billions of stars were at the center of another solar system like our own. It's difficult to conceive that there's no other life anywhere out there. If there is, it's also difficult to imagine that there's any place in the universe more beautiful and peaceful than Quetico.

Day 3

Shortly after midnight, we awoke to the sound of thunder rolling in the distance. It sounded far away, but the flashes were very intense and frequent. We wondered out loud if it was headed our way.

We decided to prepare for the worst and hope for the best. Exiting the tent and using our flashlights, we found more rope to tie the canoes to a tree so they wouldn't drift away in the storm. Previously, it had never entered my mind as to what we'd do if we became stranded on an island without our canoes. It was a sobering thought for sure and is one I still think about to this day. I suppose the only thing you could do would be to hope someone came along in another canoe, close enough to see or hear you. You could also try to make a raft of some sort and go looking for your wayward canoes, hoping to find them somewhere, blown into a shallow bay.

That thought was suddenly banished as the thunder got closer and we could see lightning flashing off to the northwest. We moved our packs into the tent and made one more circuit around the campsite to be sure nothing was left outside that we didn't want to get soaked. As the storm grew closer, it was preceded by gusty winds that whipped through the trees. This was followed shortly by big drops of rain pelting the sides of the tent.

As the storm intensified, lightning began to strike closer, accompanied by near-simultaneous claps of thunder. It was quickly upon us, and all we could do was sit on our packs and wait, hoping a tree or a branch didn't come crashing down on us. The worst of the storm lasted about 20 harrowing minutes and then began to ease as the thunder and lightning moved away to the east, and the wind shifted to come out of the northwest. It was a classic cold front passage, and I knew that tomorrow would be gusty and colder with a north wind.

As the rain lessened and then stopped altogether, the wind did the opposite. It blew harder, and the temperature dropped at least twenty degrees over the next half-hour. Anyone out in Quetico or the Minnesota Boundary Waters this night would be dealing with this. It was a rather rude reminder of how utterly powerless we are in the face of natural phenomena.

Exiting the tent to survey the campsite and check on the canoes, we found them flooded with several inches of water. We turned them over and made sure they were secured. Only a few smaller branches had come down, but everything else seemed to have weathered the storm without damage. We put our packs back outside so we could lie down again and try to sleep.

This was the first time we had to get into our sleeping bags; for the first two nights, we'd slept *on* them rather than *in* them. Following the storm, we were all wide awake, and we lay there a while discussing our trip so far.

We agreed it had been a terrific start and with the shift in temperature, tomorrow we'd probably need to wear our jeans and sweatshirts or flannels. We'd also be dealing with high winds for a change and would need to find places to fish that were sheltered on the lee side of islands. Slowly, the conversation faded, and one by one, we drifted off into a deep slumber.

After our overnight ordeal, we all slept in, finally waking around 8:00 or so. It was chilly, as first Tom, then Wayne stepped outside to see what kind of day we might have. Wayne's exclamation, "Damn, it's cold!" was all Bill and I needed to hear. We looked at each other, then turned over, burrowed deeper into our sleeping bags, and went back to sleep for another half hour or so, finally waking to the noise of pots and pans banging together as Tom and Wayne prepared coffee and a bacon and egg breakfast.

Finally emerging from the shelter of the tent, I headed straight to my pack to find my jeans and sweatshirt, socks, and dry shoes. This was going to be a very different kind of day with a brisk wind out of the northwest whipping up white caps on the lake. The sun was well up, and scuddy looking clouds with white tops and gray bottoms were racing across the sky, as if hell-bent on getting somewhere else fast.

Using our only tarp, and the rope that we'd previously used to tie our canoes to a tree overnight, we set up a windbreak between two trees. We then brought over a couple of logs to sit on while we ate. After eating in silence, just trying to stay warm, we sat with coffee cups in hand offering up opinions on what we should do today.

The options were:

1-Stay put and fish from shore around the island we were on.

2-Head out in the canoes and try to fish the lee side of the other islands in Conmee as well as the north shore which would be somewhat sheltered.

3-Forge ahead to our unnamed lake, which was much smaller and would hopefully provide more shelter from the brutal wind.

As a canoeing novice, I wasn't wild about paddling *anywhere* in those whitecaps! Yesterday, after two whole days of experience in that glassy, calm water, I fancied myself as a canoeing veteran, but this morning, looking out at the wind and waves, I reassessed my experience. I realized I was a total amateur and I didn't want any part of this wind today. I swallowed hard and kept my mouth shut, deferring to the other three and hoping they'd pick the first option. They didn't.

After a short discussion, they decided we were going to the unnamed lake as originally planned. We would have to cross about a mile of open water before arriving at a short portage into what we were now referring to as Looney Lake. There were likely dozens of "Loon Lakes" in Ontario and Minnesota, but to us, this one would forever be known as Looney Lake. So, we packed up our food, cooking utensils, and fishing gear, loaded them into the canoes, and off we went.

Tom and I led the way with him in the stern. Since our little beach was on the south side of the island, we were sheltered from the wind as we launched and headed towards the east end of the island and out into open water. I could see whitecaps out in the main lake as we approached the rocky point. The wind would be coming from our left and would be helping on the outward journey. As soon as we cleared the point, it got rough, and Tom had his hands full keeping us on track. I was just trying to keep my head down and paddle. As waves hit us from the left rear quarter, the spray came over the gunwale, and my left leg was soaked. I had my rain jacket on as a windbreaker, but I hadn't thought to put on my rain pants too. I guessed the temperature to be in the low 50's, and I just wanted this little nightmare to end soon.

With the wind at our backs, we made good time, and after about 15-20 minutes of truly miserable conditions, we approached the area where the portage should be. We couldn't wait to get out of the wind. Wayne and Bill were having a similarly tough go of it. We all got wet to one degree or another, and the wind just compounded the cold.

There was no relief from the wind until we passed a small island near the northeast tip of Conmee. The portage was supposed to be just past this island on the right side. The island gave us a little bit of shelter, and thankfully, we found the portage right where it should be. Beaching the canoes, we stepped gratefully onto dry land, relieved now that we were safely ashore. I felt like a wimp but was pleased that I hadn't bitched about their choice of taking the third option.

After scouting the portage, we found it was only about a hundred yards or so long and presented no serious challenges, like downed timber or mucky, wet bogs. We crossed it in short order and found that Looney

Lake was probably only about 150 acres in size and was indeed, considerably calmer than Conmee. There were two or three small islands that we could see from the shore, and since the end of the portage was sheltered and had some blowdowns to sit on, we opted to leave our packs there while we fished. Our intent was to catch a couple of fish for a shore lunch, wind be damned!

The sun had been in and out of the fast-moving scuddy clouds during our trip across open water. Now it was totally cloudy and, although the wind was still brisk on Looney Lake, we thought it would be manageable. Since we were still wet, we opted to build a fire and try to warm up and dry out a little before heading out to fish. Besides, a cup of hot chocolate or coffee sounded awfully good after that cold, miserable trip across Conmee. Since it had rained the night before, finding dry wood was a challenge.

There are several ways to start a fire after a rain. Since we had a small camp ax in our kit, we found a few smaller logs that we could split to get at the dry, inner sapwood. For kindling, we used pinecones which are loaded with sap, followed by small twigs that would dry quickly in the heat from the pinecones. The trick is to have plenty of fuel piled up so we could keep feeding the fire with slightly larger pieces as the fire grew hotter. Before long, we got a pretty good blaze going, and huddled closely around its warmth.

Setting some rocks around the fire as a base for the coffee pot, we soon had our choice of coffee or hot chocolate. As we warmed up both inside and out, our spirits rose as well. Looking out on the gray water, we could see it was still windy, but there were no whitecaps, and we looked forward to trying to find some fish.

After about 45 minutes around the fire, we had dried out and warmed up sufficiently to brave the wind again. Reluctantly, we doused the fire and prepped our fishing rods before climbing into the canoes to see if we could get some fish to bite after the overnight cold front. I'd always found post-cold front fishing to be a tough go.

Bill got a fish on almost immediately after we started trolling but lost it before we could even see what it was. At least it was an indication that there were fish in this lake, and some of them might be active. We trolled around the perimeter for about 45 minutes without another strike of any kind, so decided to change lures and tactics to see if we could find a formula that worked.

I suggested to Tom that we head over to the largest of Looney Lake's three islands and try casting on the lee side where we could drift without having to fight the wind so much. I tied on a medium-sized flashy, silver spoon, and Tom worked a deep running Rapala. Just off the southern tip of a rocky point, Tom got a hit. He set the hook and had a brief battle with a nice walleye that kept going deep on him. The fish weighed maybe two pounds. It was perfect for lunch and we hoped to catch another one like it. Wayne and Bill saw us land the fish and came over to see what Tom was using. They had been fishing shallow runners on the lee side of a smaller island about 100 yards or so away. Wayne had a deep running Rapala just like the one Tom was using and tied it on while Bill paddled back to their own territory.

Meanwhile, I was jigging my spoon up and down just off the bottom. I estimated we were in 15-20 feet of water when I got a vicious hit on it. The fish dove straight down then left. As I gained some line, it came towards the surface, but when it saw daylight, it headed straight back down. I got a brief glimpse of something and wasn't sure, but thought was a northern pike. After a couple of deep runs, it finally tired, and I was able to get it to the surface. It was, indeed, a pike and Tom deftly slipped the net under it and brought it aboard.

As I tried to get a grip on it, it came to life again, thrashing around the bottom of the canoe, flipping over my plastic lure organizer and fouling the net. I finally got ahold of it, but not before it raked my left thumb with its teeth and drew blood. This fish was about 28-30 inches long, so maybe 6-8 pounds. We had no desire to eat it, and it flipped out of my hands and back into the cold, gray water. Pike are especially slippery devils. It wasted no time swimming back to where it came from, and I was happy to see it go, but we still needed another walleye for lunch.

Since my thumb was bleeding, and we had left our first aid kits in the packs, we decided to head back to shore. Once ashore, Tom rifled through the packs to find a kit while I washed the cut in the lake and then stuck it under my arm to try to dry it off so we could get a bandage to stick. Tom handed me a gauze pad, and I put pressure on it while he opened a big Band-Aid. It was still oozing, so he just wrapped the Band-Aid around the gauze pad to keep some pressure on it.

Looking at my watch, I saw it was already after 1:00. We looked out on the lake and saw Bill and Wayne paddling our way. When they got within shouting distance, we asked if they'd had any luck. They had come up empty, so we had just the one fish for our shore lunch. Not wanting to mess with trying to start another fire, Wayne got out the little camp stove and fired it up. Since we still had eggs and ham, we decided to have eggs, ham, and walleye. What a great combo! It was still gray and windy, but we had some shelter and a wonderful meal. We were satisfied and began to contemplate heading back to our base camp on Conmee Lake since the fish seemed to have gone AWOL on Looney Lake.

None of us were looking forward to the trip back against wind and into the white caps, but our tent and sleeping bags were there, so we had little choice. Having cleaned our dishes and pans, we began to pack up again. Once we had everything together, we carried it all back to the Conmee side of the portage and prepared ourselves for another cold, windy paddle.

Once we cleared the small island and got back into Conmee's open water, it was a brutal 45-minute paddle. The wind was into us and quartering from the right a little bit, which tried to push us left. Wind is not a canoeist's friend. It was a real struggle for Tom and Bill (the stern paddlers) to keep the canoes headed towards our island. In the bow seats, Wayne and I paddled as hard as we could into the wind. It became a real physical challenge to continue stroking, our muscles burning from the effort. The alternative was to let the wind push us into the south shoreline, so we just sucked it up and paddled hard, testing our endurance.

We were all getting soaked again from the waves breaking over the gunwales, and I don't ever recall being so physically miserable. It took us almost three times as long to get back as it did to get to Looney Lake. Once we arrived on the lee side of our island, we were totally exhausted, and we could hardly pull the canoes up onto the narrow beach. Our hands were so cold we could barely move our fingers, and all we wanted to do was get out of that damned wind, get a fire going and warm up.

Once we secured the canoes and took the cooking and food packs out, we all made for our own packs to find dry clothes. Each of us having only brought one pair of jeans, which were now soaking wet, we were forced to put on shorts. After changing, we all pitched in to gather wood and kindling; getting a fire started right away was imperative!

We re-secured our windbreak and got a fire going, then Tom and I went searching for more fuel. By now it was after 4:00, so we needed a hefty pile of firewood in order to keep that fire going all evening,

With a steady blaze established, we hung our jeans on sticks like hot dogs, and held them to the flames trying to dry them out without catching them on fire! As the legs dried out, steam rose off them. What a change it had been from just 24 hours earlier when we were warm and dry, looking forward to a beautiful evening ahead. Things can change quickly in Quetico. In only three days, we'd experienced the park at its best and near its worst. I wasn't sure what could be worse than what we'd been through today, but I'm sure other visitors to this wilderness have seen sleet and snow, especially in the spring or fall. Once we got our jeans dry, we all changed again, and felt a lot better after having some rest and warm, dry, clothes to wear.

My experience told me that after a strong cold front comes through, high-pressure generally builds in behind it. High-pressure systems rotate clockwise, indicating that this north wind we were having was the front side of the high. If the system got directly over us, we should have light, variable winds, followed in a day or two by southerly winds from the backside of the high and that would mean warmer weather to come. That was my prediction, and the guys hoped I was right!

At about 6:00 or so, we started getting hungry again and had a desire for walleye. Having shared just one small fish for lunch, we felt we had been cheated, so decided to see if we could catch anything from the shore. None of us wanted anything more to do with canoes on this day, so we grabbed our rods and favorite lures and split up, heading for different parts of the island, avoiding the north side altogether. After about 45 minutes without any success, I headed back to camp where I happily found Tom and Wayne cleaning a walleye and a smallmouth bass. Bill wandered back about 15 minutes later and said he'd caught a small pike, but that was it.

We were famished after the workout we had trying to get back to camp earlier this afternoon and discussed what to have with the fish. We unanimously voted for fried potatoes and oddly enough, Bill had a thing for pancakes. So... we had pancakes, walleye, smallmouth, and fried potatoes. Another great combo as it turned out. I'd never eaten so much in my life, but with the fresh air and vigorous exercise I was getting, I felt stronger and fitter than I had in years.

By the time we finished eating, the sun began to show itself now and then in glimpses behind the trees, offering a warm glow in the western sky. It was still mostly cloudy, but the wind was letting up and the air smelled clean and fresh. As the fire was dying, we made hot chocolate and soaked up the last of the warmth from the remaining embers while reflecting on the harshness of this day. There would be no stargazing tonight. It was getting chilly, but hopefully, tomorrow would bring more sunshine and lighter winds. The sleeping bags felt especially good tonight as we settled in.

Day 4

We each began to stir as the skies lightened, and the birds began their day. A pair of jays were having a domestic dispute in the trees above the tent, and the chipmunks and red squirrels were arguing over an odd seed or nut somewhere close by. I laid there for a few more minutes in the warmth of my sleeping bag, eyes closed, listening as our island woke up.

I hadn't previously paid much attention to the background sounds of Quetico, having been so distracted by its visual beauty. For the creatures who called this place home, it was just another day as they went about their daily routines of life and survival. No doubt, some would not live to see another day as they became prey and sustenance for something a little higher up the food chain. This is the way of nature and I was thankful to be immersed in it for a while longer before I had to return to my own daily routine. I suddenly missed Mary Jane and the kids. I wanted them to know and feel what I was so fortunate to experience this week. Today would mark the halfway point in our adventure.

My little reverie was broken as I heard Tom unzip his sleeping bag, then sit up with a loud yawn. He undid the tent flap and stuck his head out.

"The wind has died down." he said. The sun wasn't quite up yet, but the sky was clear with a few clouds floating overhead... and it was COLD. Not "frosty" cold, but it felt like the temperature had dropped into the forties overnight because of the clearing sky and building high pressure. It looked like we were in for a much nicer day, a delightful change from yesterday's brutal wind and whitecaps. As we exited the warmth of our sleeping bags and the tent, we quickly began digging in our packs for sweatshirts and socks. The crisp morning was very reminiscent of October in Michigan.

Opening the food packs, we discovered we were running low on eggs...only five left! Should we save them for tomorrow? Nope, we were going to finish the eggs and ham this morning. The only way to split five eggs equitably amongst four guys was to scramble them. We still had enough bacon for one or two more meals.

Then Bill had a brilliant idea. We still had plenty of bread, so we could make French toast. We had no milk but could whip up the eggs and mix them with a little lake water to thin it out, then dip the bread in the mixture and pop them in the frying pan with butter. We'd been making pancakes with a batter made with water, so why not French toast? The pancakes had kind of an odd texture, but we thought they were still pretty good. So, French toast it was, and it was damned good. Amazing what a little butter and real maple syrup can do. The sweetness of the French toast and syrup combined with the salty fried ham was very satisfying.

As we sat around drinking coffee, we discussed the plans for the day. The wind was still out of the north, but not nearly as strong as yesterday. I was pessimistic about how the fishing would be with a north wind, but all we needed to catch were a few fish for lunch and for dinner.

Conmee was a big lake with many islands, and there were some small streams feeding into it, so there were plenty of places that should hold fish. The trick today would be patience and trying different lures and different depths to see if we could coax some of them into striking.

Since we would be spending another night here, we had all day to explore the lake and try to find some fish. We cleaned up our dishes and pans, drank one last cup of coffee, doused the fire, then tidied up the camp and hung our remaining food out of reach of bears. The plan for the day was to split up and fish different areas, then meet back at base camp between noon and 1:00 for what we hoped would be a walleye or lake trout lunch. We could then compare notes about what worked and what didn't.

Tom and I decided to go south. There was a lot of promising water in south Conmee, short of the portage into Suzanette Lake. Wayne and Bill would head to the north shore, where there were numerous coves and inlets as well as lots of islands. We all shoved off about 8:00am.

It was still breezy from the north, so Tom and I had a nice little tailwind. We trolled as we slowly paddled, merely enjoying the beauty and solitude. The frantic pace of yesterday was gone. The sun was warm on our faces, and it was a beautiful but cool day. As we rounded a point, we saw another eagle in the distance, basking in the warm sun at the top of a tree, just as a flock of cormorants took off in loose formation, two feet off the water headed west. Cormorants are odd-looking birds. While geese and ducks have longer necks, cormorants have shorter, thicker necks with shorter wings about halfway between their heads and tails. They also like to sit in trees and are great divers. They've been known to dive more than 100 feet in search of their prey of minnows and small fish.

We still hadn't seen a moose. Tom said they had just been unlucky because they'd talked to a lot of outfitters and other campers over the years who said moose sightings were commonplace. We all hoped that this would be the year.

We were sliding quietly along in a calm cove when Tom got a hit on his shallow running Rapala. It was a smallmouth that jumped almost immediately and spit the lure right back in our faces. It hit the side of the canoe with a loud metallic bang. It was a good sign though that some fish were active. Since we hadn't had a trout for lunch or dinner yet, we were hoping we'd catch one today. We put our lures back in the water and kept paddling at a leisurely pace. As we got closer to the eagle, it became uncomfortable with our proximity and gracefully left its observation post to disappear behind the trees.

I was thinking back to yesterday when everything we did was hard work. We were so busy and so miserable that we hardly took note of our surroundings. Today was much different, and we appreciated every little thing we saw, even the way the sunlight was filtering through the trees. In this quiet little cove, out of the wind, it was so warm and inviting I could have easily laid back and taken a nap.

We continued trolling as we slowly paddled out of the cove and into a narrows between the left shoreline and a small island to our right. Just as we hit the slot, Tom got another fish on. This one didn't come up, but fought deep and hard, more like a trout or walleye... or a pike. We were hoping it wasn't a pike. I reeled in my spoon and had the net ready as Tom fought the fish, which appeared to be a pretty good one judging from the bend in the rod. He gained some line as he tried to bring the fish to the surface. We kept peering over the side where the line entered the water, trying to see what it was but before we could get a glimpse, it dove deep again, stripping line from Tom's reel as the drag whirred. I told him that this was probably not a walleye. It had to be a big trout or a big northern. If it was a walleye, it was huge.

Once again, Tom began to get some line back, this time getting the fish near the canoe where it swam underneath to the other side. We both turned around to the other side and saw it was, indeed, a big fish... but alas, a pike. We were a little disappointed it wasn't a lake trout, but it gave Tom a good fight. Rather than net this one, I grabbed a needle nose pliers and grasped the hook. One quick twist and the fish was free. It wasted no time diving away, out of sight into the clear depths of Conmee Lake.

It was now after 10:00am, and we still didn't have a fish for lunch. We hoped Wayne and Bill were having better luck, but at least Tom had caught a nice fish and had another one on briefly before spitting the hook. Once we passed the south tip of the island, we came upon a surreal sight. There was another small island behind it, maybe 200 yards long and only about 50 yards wide... that was *totally blackened.* By that I mean it was burned to a crisp. A fire had consumed everything on the entire island right to the waterline. We paddled all the way around it looking for even a sprig of green growth, any sign of life, and saw none. It must have been recent. Had it been last year, or even earlier this spring, I'm sure something green would have sprouted by now.

We pulled the canoe up onto the shore and got out to walk around. We wanted to see if we could find any clue at all as to what had happened. Everything was simply charred and black. There were only two explanations, one being a lightning strike, and the other being a man-made fire, either by accident or intentional. We couldn't imagine why anyone would deliberately set an island on fire in this beautiful, pristine wilderness. After walking through the charred remains of trees, branches, and grasses, we got back into the canoe, shaking our heads in bewilderment. We preferred to believe it was a lightning strike, which would be a totally natural phenomenon. It was visually striking for its stark contrast to the beautiful, green landscape as far as we could see in every other direction.

As we paddled away from the charred island, we continued to troll, intending to fish our way back in the direction of the base camp. Maybe we could come up with something for lunch. If we failed to catch anything, and the other two had struck out as well, we'd probably have to break out the peanut butter. We still had some spaghetti, bread, and several potatoes along with maybe a half-pound of bacon, pancake mix, flour and a couple of jars of peanut butter. But with four days left, we'd need to catch some fish, or we'd be ravenous by the time we got back to civilization.

We headed west across some open water. The wind was still northerly and was beginning to pick up a little, adding some chill to the air as we left the shelter of the islands, although it was nothing like yesterday. We didn't get any action crossing the open water, but we were approaching what appeared to be a rock pile sticking out of the water. As we got closer, we saw that it was a kind of shoal that was a couple of hundred feet in diameter and tapered into the depths around all sides. This looked like promising water for a walleye or maybe a lake trout. Fish like to relate to structure of some kind, and this really fit the bill. These kinds of rocky shoals seemed to be quite common and were simply rocky islands that were barely high enough to break the surface of the water.

We decided to fish all around the perimeter. Tom was casting a Rapala, and I was jigging a Johnson Silver Minnow as we alternately paddled, drifted, then paddled again, slowly working our way around the rocky outcrop. As we moved around the south side of the formation, I got a pretty good thump on my Johnson spoon, I set the hook and brought a nice 2-pound walleye to the surface. Tom netted it, and we put it on a stringer. If necessary, this would feed all four of us for lunch. We continued to work the same depth, which I estimated to be 15-20 feet, all the way around the rock pile and then worked it again a little deeper this time. I hooked another walleye, this one a little smaller than the first, though with these two fish, we had plenty for lunch. It was a little after 11:00 when we decided to head back to base camp. If Bill and Wayne weren't back yet, we'd go ahead and fillet the two fish and await their return before breaking out the cooking gear. I told Tom I was ready for a nap, and he agreed.

Paddling against the north breeze, it took us about a half-hour to reach the base camp. Bill and Wayne hadn't yet returned, so we filleted the two walleyes, put them in the frying pan and covered them with a tarp both to keep the bugs off as well as hide them from the ghostly gulls that appeared out of thin air, like apparitions, whenever we cleaned fish. I wondered where the gulls came from. I never noticed them until we cleaned fish. It was as if they were hiding behind trees and watching... and waiting.

I retrieved my air mattress from the tent and found a sunny spot where I could stretch out on the island's south side, out of the breeze. Tom did the same. I pulled my cap down over my eyes, and we chatted for a few minutes. The conversation quickly tapered off, and we fell sound asleep within minutes.

We awoke suddenly to excited shouting, "Look at the size of that thing!" and "holy shit, that's a monster!" Tom and I had been out like a light. Confused and startled, we looked around frantically for the source of all the noise. Then the laughter started. Bill and Wayne had seen us sleeping as they approached the little beach.

"Assholes!" Tom and I replied in unison. We didn't see the humor in it. We'd been sound asleep for maybe 15 minutes and woke up grouchy. They didn't have a fish on, in fact, they hadn't caught anything all morning. We told them we'd been "skunked" too and would have to break out the peanut butter. We waited for them to pull their canoe up on the beach and get out and stretch. They were tired, too, but we weren't about to let them rest. Since we were all hungry, we suggested they go get the sandwich fixings out. We waited until they got the food packs down from the ropes and dug everything out and began making their sandwiches before uncovering the frying pan with the walleye fillets. They looked at us with disgust and said, "Assholes!"

Having evened the score, we all laughed and began working together to put on a feast for lunch. We did the fried potato, pan-fried walleye combo that really defines a proper shore lunch in these cold northern waters of the Canadian Shield. While we ate, Tom and I related our experience with the charred island and how we think it must have started. Bill and Wayne found it very interesting and agreed that it must have been a lightning strike. It's certainly what we *wanted* to believe.

After lunch and after we'd cleaned up our pans and utensils, we all felt lethargic and listless. I think the whole experience was catching up to us. We'd all been on a natural "high" for weeks, beginning with the excitement and anticipation of planning the trip, packing, leaving home, meeting in Duluth, arriving in Ely, flying into Lac La Croix, and experiencing so many wondrous things over the last few days. All of that combined with the brutally difficult day we had yesterday, fighting the wind, cold weather, and getting soaked during our open water crossings, had taken its toll on us.

We agreed, at least for the time being, to just hang around the camp for the afternoon. The sun was shining brightly, the wind had died down to a gentle breeze, the birds were singing, and we were just plain tired. I went back to my air mattress and tried to finish my nap. You can never go back and "finish" a nap. You either have a nap, or you don't. I'd already had a nap. I just didn't finish it because I'd been so rudely awakened. I was still tired, but not sleepy, so I decided to explore the island a little further. Having canoed around it, I figured it was nearly a mile long by about a half-mile wide, so a pretty sizeable piece of land. I doubted that there were any resident bears, but I kept my eyes and ears open just in case.

Walking quietly, I tried to tread upon rocks rather than twigs. Being part of the Canadian Shield meant that there was a lot more rock than soil in this area. Plant life struggled to get a foothold, and when it did, it held on for dear life! So many gnarled tree roots curled over rocks to find anchorage in the sparse soil from which to gain nutrients and water. The Shield extends from the Great Lakes all the way to the Arctic Ocean in a U shape going around Hudson Bay. Millions of years ago, there were very young and very high, mountain peaks on this part of the planet. Erosion and glacial movement knocked them down to gentle hills and scoured the rock faces over many millennia.

Some of the more prevalent mammals that call Quetico home are white-tailed deer, moose, black bears, beavers, river otters, mink, foxes, gray wolves, lynx, and coyotes. From a distance, we'd seen what we thought was an otter and something quite small swimming which could have been a mink. We'd seen lots of deer drinking the pure cold water, though still no bears or moose. Tom had said we'd probably see a beaver at some point, or at least some beaver dams, on our way back through the Darky River. Current maps show the names were changed at some point in the last 30 years or so to the Dark Water River and Dark Water Lake. I haven't been able to find out exactly when or why the changes were made. I'm referring to them here by the names that appear on my map which was printed in 1971.

As I slowly walked our island, I heard birds singing but had trouble seeing and identifying them. I heard woodpeckers, rat-a-tat-tatting on some hollow trees in the distance, jays arguing nearby, and chickadees singing their customary chickadee-dee-dee and flitting about in the pines. Eastern chipmunks and red squirrels scurried about among the debris of pinecones and twigs looking for morsels. There was a lot of life on this island, most of which I would never see. I saw just the quick, flashy movement. But what of the other life on this island both big and small...

very small, like insects, spiders and voles? There was an entire ecosystem that lived, found food, water and shelter, and reproduced and died only on this island.

That thought made me recall this morning's walk on the small charred island. It looked dead, but it wasn't *totally* dead. It would one day come back to life as living organisms beneath the surface that had survived the fire would begin to sprout as rain penetrated the soil. Birds would carry seeds in their droppings. There are some species of conifers that will only release the seeds from their cones as a result of the intense heat of a fire. This unique condition is known as *serotiny* and is the result of the seeds in the cones being coated with a very hard resin which melts during a fire and releases the seeds. It's nature's way of regenerating a forest after a wildfire. The island would turn green again and the cycle of life would go on as it has for millions of years.

As I roamed back in the general direction of our camp, I started picking up dry branches for our evening campfire. When I got back, I had a real armload and was happy to drop it next to the fire pit. Tom and Wayne were napping, so Bill and I grabbed our favorite fishing rods and headed for the rocky point on the east end, about a hundred yards away.

We carefully navigated some downed timber, and then some bowling ball sized rocks before coming up on a huge boulder. There was a perfect looking flat area to fish from on the other side, but it meant either wading ankle-deep around it or climbing over it to get there. It was a clumsy climb for me, so I opted to wade. Bill was taller than me by 6 or 7 inches, and had no trouble climbing up onto the boulder. I had dry shoes back in the camp so what the hell, off I went, feeling my way. It was much muckier than it appeared, and I stepped right out of my left shoe. Now I'm standing on one foot, with a fishing rod in one hand feeling down in the mud for my shoe with the other. "How about a hand?" I asked, as I tried to give Bill my fishing rod. He responded with a short round of applause. I said, "Jerk!" and then lost my balance and fell, butt-first, into about a half-foot of water. This brought a roar of laughter from Bill. He finally recovered enough to grab my rod, then my hand, and pulled me up. I finally found my shoe and recovered it with a giant sucking sound. Swishing it in the water to clean the mud out, I threw it up on the boulder. I finally got around to the flat spot and sat on a smaller rock and put my shoe back on.

Now that the drama and humor had subsided, we set about casting to both sides of the rocky point in search of dinner. After a dozen or so unsuccessful casts, we decided to venture a little further out on the point by carefully stepping from rock to rock. The further out we went, the fewer dry rocks we had in front of us. I was already soaked, so I had no problem getting a little further out, but the rocks underfoot were now submerged...and getting slippery. I had trouble maintaining solid footing and ended up flailing around trying to keep my balance. I must admit, it must have been comical to watch as I heard laughter coming from the trees. Tom and Wayne had apparently come back to life and joined us in trying to catch a fish for dinner.

I carefully made my way back towards the safety of the shoreline, while my buddies were casually casting away, not really caring if they caught anything or not. We were just four guys out in the middle of nowhere enjoying each other's company. The water was blue, the trees were green, and a loon was calling in the distance. It was now late afternoon, and the sun was warm on our faces. The wind had died down to a gentle breeze now, and life in Quetico was beautiful once again.

Having had an excellent walleye and fried potato shore lunch today, we really didn't care much if we caught anything for dinner. We half-heartedly tried different lures, lost a couple of them in the rocks, and never got a fish on. We could have taken the canoes out and tried harder, but none of us had much enthusiasm for it.

Randomly, we returned to the camp and fussed around with our packs, jotted notes in our journals and began preparing our gear to head out tomorrow, down into Brent Lake, then back into the south end of Darky Lake where we would see some of the ancient pictographs. I was feeling a little melancholy that we were already having to head back, but also excited that we still had four more days with some new territory to see on the return trip. It was decided we'd have spaghetti with just butter and salt for dinner, which turned out to be very satisfying.

With the sun setting on day four, we heated some water for hot chocolate and broke out the Oreos. We gathered our air mattresses and went out on the big rock, fifteen feet above
the waterline and sat watching the sky darken and the stars begin to magically appear. It was a magnificent, crystal-clear night. We watched again for satellites and hoped to see the northern lights, but it wasn't to be this night. It was getting chilly, and we sat quietly for another fifteen minutes or so before reluctantly heading for the tent and the warmth of our sleeping bags. It had been another good day.

Day 5

Awakening at dawn, we began the daily ritual of checking the weather by sticking our heads out of the tent. It was dead calm this morning, and it was also extremely foggy. This was a first for us on this trip. The fog was so dense we couldn't see the canoes from thirty feet away. It was also beautiful in the way it made our immediate world so small, smothering sound like a blanket.

Emerging from the tent, we stretched, took a deep breath of fresh, moist Canadian air, then addressed our immediate needs first by heading off in four different directions. With the thick fog, we didn't have to go very far to be out of sight of the camp. That also meant that none of us could actually *see* the camp. After we took care of our personal business, we all found our way back except for Wayne. After a few minutes we heard "Hey, where the hell is the camp?" coming from the gray void. He sounded further away than he should have and seemed to be wandering in the wrong direction.

Tom called "Over here!". Then Wayne yelled back, "Keep talking so I know what direction I'm going!" We kept yelling "Over here" until we heard his footsteps breaking twigs. Finally, he emerged from the trees like an apparition. When he saw us, he said, "That was really spooky!"

Once back in camp, we set about making a fire for coffee and a pancake breakfast. We figured we'd also better finish the last of the bacon before it spoiled. We knew we weren't going anywhere until the fog lifted, so we weren't in any hurry. With a good fire going and coffee mugs in hand, we spread out our maps and planned the day's route. We were going back to the western end of Conmee, then south through several nameless lakes and rivers. We intended to reach Brent Lake by evening if the fog lifted in time for us to get a decent start. According to my watch, the sun had been up for about a half-hour, though the fog still hung heavily on the camp.

There were two portages marked by our outfitter between Conmee and Brent. Tom and the guys had never gone that way, so we didn't know if they'd be tough ones or not. The first one looked like it would be about a third of a mile, maybe a half-mile at most. The second seemed to be only about half that, so with a little luck it would be an easy day of paddling with a couple of interruptions for some exercise. We hadn't done any serious portaging for three days now. We put the frying pan on the fire, and Bill put the last of the bacon on while I mixed the pancake batter.

While eating, we reminisced about the first half of the trip. According to our outfitter, this second half would be different in that we wouldn't have as much open water as we'd had while paddling through McAree to Wicksteed and William, then into Conmee. The nameless lakes on this route were smaller, narrower and offered a better chance of seeing a moose!

By the time we finished eating, it was getting a bit lighter, and the fog had some bright spots in it. The trees were dripping with beads of water from the fog, and when it lifted enough for a little sunshine to penetrate, they shone like diamonds. It was short-lived but stunning and is one of my favorite mental images from the trip. The fog was burning off quickly as the sun rose a little higher in the sky. It looked like it was going to be another gorgeous day. The air was fresh and crisp, the sky was blue, and the lake was like a mirror with little wisps of leftover fog hovering near the shoreline.

After cleaning our pans and utensils, we began breaking down the tent. Our backpacks were now noticeably lighter than they'd been a few days ago. We'd consumed nearly all the perishables by now and were going to need to rely more heavily on catching some fish and eating the few potatoes we had left. We still had some spaghetti, bread, peanut butter, and an unopened package of Oreos. Also, we still had an ample supply of instant coffee and a dozen or so packets of hot chocolate... plus all the freshwater we could drink!

Once we finished packing, we carefully loaded the canoes. Pouring the remaining water from the coffee pot onto the fire, we then refilled it, stirred the ashes and doused it again, making sure the fire was completely out. The sight of the charred island yesterday renewed our determination that we would NEVER be responsible for a wildfire.

After walking the campsite again to be sure we were leaving nothing behind that hadn't been there when we arrived, we launched the canoes and headed west. Tom invited me to retake the stern, and I gladly accepted.

The canoes were well balanced and easy to steer on the mirror-like surface of this calm, clear morning. It was about 9:30, the sun was getting higher and was warm on our backs as we paddled in the fresh air. I never tired of the wild beauty of this place. The scenery was similar but was also changing constantly as we paddled past different islands and found new picture postcards around every new bend.

The beautiful silence of paddling a canoe allowed the senses to be on the alert to sounds and movement in the trees and along the shorelines. When we started out 5 days ago, I was a noisy, novice canoe paddler. Now I took a lot of pride in how quietly I paddled. It was second nature to my buddies who'd been doing this for years. For me, it was a new skill in which I took a lot of pride. Much like riding a bike, I can still do it today.

Approaching the western end of Conmee, we stopped to check our navigation, making sure of the point where we needed to turn south towards the first of the two portages. We were all in agreement and continued around a large island before heading into a narrows that led to the first portage. Approaching from the north, we had little trouble finding it and pulled the canoes ashore. Scouting the path, this turned out to be even shorter than it appeared on our maps and it went around some beautiful rapids. We stopped and admired the view a little before hefting the canoes and packs.

It was an easy portage, so when we went back for the remaining backpacks, we stopped to play in the rapids like little kids. We'd put a stick in at the top end and try to follow it down to see if it would make it to the bottom without getting hung up on something. It brought back so many childhood memories of playing in streams and ditches after rainstorms without a care in the world. We lost ourselves in this little paradise for about a half-hour before finally heading back to finish the portage and move on.

Launching the canoes again, we found ourselves in a beautiful, narrow passage paddling towards the second portage. We trolled this narrows as we paddled but never had a hit. Several deer were drinking in one spot near a small clearing. All of them appeared to be does since bucks would have mature antlers by this time of the year. Oddly, deer antlers are the fastest growing bone known. Depending on the health of the deer and the quality of its food source, a white-tailed deer's antlers can grow up to a quarter inch per day from late March to early August. We also saw another eagle flying high overhead. This portion felt like a very long, narrow lake of its own, pinched at both ends, one of which we already portaged and the second of which we were now approaching. It was easy to find, and as we beached the canoes, we saw that this one was going to start sharply uphill.

Tom and I took the canoes and got right to work. I wasn't getting any better at this but remained full of determination to carry my weight. As before, I struggled to get the bulky beast balanced with the yoke on my shoulders. Bill helped me as Tom had already begun the uphill trek. I wobbled a bit at the start but finally got into a rhythm just putting one foot in front of the other. The trail eventually leveled out a bit, then towards the end started steeply downhill. The footing was dry but going downhill with that load on my back was scary!

I tried not to think of the consequences of taking a spill at this point and just concentrated hard on taking it slow and watching my footing. Tom was already at the end when I arrived and helped me get the canoe off my back. Bill and Wayne were right behind me, and we stopped to rest in the shade awhile before heading back. This portage was shorter than the last one but was much more difficult because of the elevation changes. Once we'd regained our strength, we hiked back for the rest of our gear and then returned and launched out into Brent Lake.

Back home in Michigan, there were thousands of inland lakes, but nearly all of them were distinguished by the fact that they were mostly isolated from other lakes. There were some lake chains connected by rivers or streams, but most were deep puddles of fifty to a few hundred acres in size that were the result of glaciation but lacked the granite and metamorphic rock formations that formed the Canadian Shield.

Here in Quetico, and the Minnesota Boundary Waters, these lakes went on forever and nearly all were connected in some way to each other. On the map, Brent Lake was huge, though not big and round.

It went on for miles in narrows and broader sections, broken up by hundreds of islands, big and small. It was little wonder that while some of these bodies of water were named, many were not since it seemed impossible to determine where one ended, and another began. It all appeared so arbitrary, and I wondered how they were named. Was there a "Brent" somewhere? Who was McAree? Was William named after someone's kid? According to our maps, especially to the north of us, many of the lakes had odd names, such as "Wink Lake" and "That Lake" and "Jack Lake" and even "Your Lake". It would be fascinating to know how and why they got their names.

Once we launched into Brent, we again had to pay close attention to our navigation so as not to become hopelessly lost. Looking at a map is vastly different than what you see at water level from a canoe. What looked like an uninterrupted shoreline from a distance turned out to be two or three islands. Brent Lake seemed different from the lakes we'd encountered in the first four days because it was so broken up into bays and islands, both big and small.

There was a long portage between Brent and Darky that we would navigate tomorrow, and we wanted to camp somewhere close to that tonight. From here, we could get back to Lac La Croix in a carefree two days if necessary, so there was no need to rush. Brent was a beautiful place as we seemed to always be in close proximity to a shoreline. There were not as many big expanses of open water as we had in McAree and especially in Wicksteed and William.

It was now early afternoon, and we decided to troll Brent as we made our way generally west. If we caught a couple of walleyes early on, we'd stop for a shore lunch somewhere. It was a perfect August day as we drifted quietly while enjoying nature at its finest. About fifteen minutes later, as we passed the tip of an island, I got a hit on my deep-diving River Runt. Everyone reeled in to avoid entanglements and watched as I brought a nice smallmouth bass up to the boat. We decided to release it in hopes of finding a walleye or a lake trout. Continuing to troll, Bill got a hit on his favorite deep-running Rapala. This one fought deep, so we knew it was a walleye, a laker, or a pike.

After a five-minute battle, Wayne netted a beautiful lake trout of about four pounds. This was just what we'd hoped for. It would yield a couple of big fillets that would finally satisfy that desire for a trout lunch we'd had for several days. Heading for the nearest shoreline, we scouted for a suitable place to beach the canoes that also had some flat rocks nearby where we could setup the camp stove and prepare a meal. It didn't take us long to find a great spot and we pulled the canoes up onto a narrow, sandy beach.

Since we wouldn't be staying overnight, we didn't want to start a campfire, so as Bill filleted the trout, Wayne set up the Coleman stove and I sliced up one potato. This would be a simple lunch of fresh, pan-fried trout with a couple of bites of fried potato. It didn't get much simpler or much better than this. I sat there on a flat rock in the August sun, enjoying a wonderful trout lunch, and silently thanked my lucky stars that Tom had called me back in early May. I was having the time of my life!

After a leisurely meal, we cleaned our pans and found a couple of flat places to stretch out and rest a bit. None of us really napped, but just relaxed and enjoyed the warmth for twenty minutes or so while we chatted. Although we had more paddling ahead, we had no need or desire to hurry. Casually, we packed up the cooking gear and studied our maps again before setting out.

This time Tom took the stern, and I planted myself in the bow. We had a plan. The route we'd chosen would take us around a big bend to the south and then even a little southeast before curving back westward again towards the long portage into Darky. We should be able to find a suitable campsite in the southwest part of Brent, leaving us less than an hour from the portage which we'd tackle tomorrow morning.

It was now a little after 2:00, and it was getting hot as we paddled. There was little or no breeze reaching us in these canyons of trees and rock faces. There were even some sheer granite walls extending 10-20 feet high in some places. Tom said the pictographs in south Darky Lake were on similar walls where you could paddle right up to them and take pictures. I was really looking forward to seeing them tomorrow.

Trolling as we went, we caught a fish every now and then, mostly smallmouths and a couple of walleyes. We released them all but wondered later if we should have kept a couple for dinner. Still satisfied from our trout lunch, it was just a casual afterthought until we realized it was now coming up on 5:00 and we should start looking for a suitable campsite and a proper dinner.

We'd now been out for five days and still hadn't seen another canoe, even at a distance. It was astounding to me that this place was so accessible yet so remote and void of people. It's a testament to how this wonderful resource is managed by the Canadian Parks Ministry and the U.S. Department of the Interior.

As our route began to change from a southeastern track, back more to the southwest, the lake started to open into bigger water. It was still sunny and bright, but off to the east, we could see it was raining way off in the distance. It looked like a couple of miles away, and there was a perfect double rainbow. Digging our cameras out of our packs, we took lots of pictures, but we found later, as with the eagle photos, they didn't do justice to the moment. Weather in this part of the world generally moves west to east, so we were in no danger of getting wet from that particular pop-up shower, but it was a beautiful sight to see.

Paddling on towards the southwest and hugging the northwest shoreline, we kept an eye out for a good place to camp for the night. After rejecting a couple of locations, we found one that looked suitable from the water and beached the canoes for a closer look. It was very much like the site we'd had on Conmee and had a great, flat tent pad and a ready-made circle of stones that had seen a lot of use over the years.

Having unanimously agreed that this was near perfect, we unloaded our gear and piled it all in a heap. We really wanted a walleye dinner and decided to get back in the now-empty canoes and do some serious fishing. There were multiple "fishy" looking places nearby with rocky points and shoals. A couple of small islands also looked like they might hold fish off some deep pools bordered by boulders.

Tom and I headed for a quiet cove surrounded by several big boulders, optimistic about our chances. Sometimes you just get a good feeling about a spot. Tom hooked a good fish on his third cast which turned out to be a three-pound walleye. That would make dinner even if we didn't get another one. Shortly after that, I hooked one of about equal size, and just like that, a good dinner was assured. We began to wonder if Wayne and Bill were having any luck. We'd only been out for about 30 minutes so we decided to paddle around the point to see if we could see them. We did, just as Bill was netting another walleye that Wayne had just caught. We paddled up and showed them our catch. All three fish were similar in size, and we decided to keep all three and fillet them out. We'd have half for dinner tonight and the other half for breakfast tomorrow.
Beaching the canoes, Tom and I set about filleting the three fish. We put the raw fillets in a pan of cold water and covered them. The gulls appeared again from wherever they hide, having another raucous fight over the carcasses.

Since none of us had bathed since the evening before the cold front passed, we were all getting a little ripe. We also needed to do our laundry. There was an enormous boulder, cresting about five feet above the waterline, just to the left of the place we'd beached the canoes. Tom was a very strong swimmer, so he waded in and dove to be sure the water was deep enough to jump off the boulder without bottoming out. He popped up and said he couldn't find the bottom, so Bill climbed up on the big rock and did a perfect cannonball with water flying everywhere. I followed, and then Wayne.

The water was freezing at first, but we got used to it in short order and did several more leaps from the big rock. Between jumps, we gathered some of our clothes from the past two days and threw them in, scrubbing them in the cold clear water, then wringing them out and tossing them up on the big rock before getting in a few last dog paddles.

This really revived us after a hot day of paddling and portaging. We had also reacquired our appetites after burning off our trout lunch from earlier and were ready for some walleye. After stringing a clothesline, we hung up our wet clothes and got into the last of our clean, dry ones. We all had some work to do setting up the tent, gathering firewood, getting the cooking gear out, and getting the fire started.

After five days together, we were working well as a team. We all knew what had to be done and how to do it, whether it was filleting fish, setting up the tent, starting a fire, preparing meals or cleaning the pots and pans afterward. I really felt like I was pulling my weight and contributing to the success of the trip, and it was very gratifying.

When we lived in Wisconsin before our kids were born, Mary Jane and I had done a little camping in the northern part of the state, around Minocqua and Tomahawk, but this was vastly different.

The summer before our first son Jamie was born, we'd spent a single night on Trout Lake north of Minocqua with our little 12-foot aluminum boat and 6hp Evinrude outboard. We had our little dog, Abbey, a Benjie type mutt, with us. We got chased off the mainland to a nearby island by a skunk that decided to explore our campsite in the middle of the night. We heard rustling in the leaves and twigs outside the tent, though not like a bear or anything big. Abbey was on full alert, not barking, but emitting a low menacing growl. Not knowing what was out there, I found my flashlight and poked my head out of the tent flap expecting to see a raccoon. "Oh shit!" I said. Mary Jane said, "What?!" "It's a skunk!" I replied. Obviously, dogs and skunks don't mix well.

I slowly exited the tent, trying to encourage the varmint to leave without pissing it off. It eventually wandered harmlessly off into the darkness, but we lay there for another half hour, wide awake now, listening to every little night sound. Abbey was still on the alert and whining, acting like she wanted to go outside. Deciding it was like waiting for the other shoe to drop, we resigned ourselves to breaking down the tent and loading it, the cooler, the sleeping bags, the dog and the rest of our gear into our little 12 footer and motoring about 300 yards out to the larger of three small islands.

There was no moon that night, so I stationed Mary Jane in the bow with our Coleman Lantern, looking like George Washington crossing the Delaware. That pretty much put an end to our family camping adventures!

About thirty minutes after starting our chores, we had walleye fillets sizzling in the pan along with a couple of potatoes. We felt clean again, we had coffee in our mugs and were just enjoying each other's company around a wilderness campfire.

Although I'd met Wayne once before, a very long time ago, I'd never met Bill until they picked me up in Duluth. That seemed so long ago, though it had only been a little less than a week. Even so, we had all developed a real camaraderie. We had gotten to know each other well and enjoyed each other's company. This trip was turning out exactly as I'd hoped it would.

Following dinner and our cleanup chores, we lounged around the camp, writing in our journals or reading until it became too dark to continue. We stoked the fire enough to get some hot water for our evening hot chocolate ritual so that we could go sit up on the rocks and gaze into the endless universe. Was there intelligent life out there somewhere looking back at us and wondering the same? It was difficult to imagine that there wasn't. We counted satellites again, coming up with three this time. It was fascinating to see them, like moving stars, all on different orbits.

The northern horizon was hidden behind the trees so we couldn't tell if the northern lights were putting on a show tonight. I'd seen them twice when living in central Wisconsin, pulsing bands of greenish light that radiated from the horizon to overhead. Tomorrow we'd try to find a campsite with a view of the northern sky. So far, we had been very fortunate on this trip having such beautiful, clear skies at night. When I was preparing for this adventure, the magic of cloudless night skies never entered my mind.

Yawning nearly in unison, we retired to the tent for the fifth time this week.

Day 6

We awoke on day six to cloudy skies and calm winds. It was a mild, humid morning and smelled like rain. Although it was dry, we thought we might be in for some precipitation at some point today, hoping that it might hold off until tonight, but doubtful that it would.

Now that we were on the homeward leg, I realized that crystal clear nights like we'd had last night, laying out on my back, staring straight up into the endless universe would be one of my most treasured memories of all. When we started this trip on Saturday it was a new moon, so the sky was very dark. Now, nearly a week later, it was a waxing crescent, so it still wasn't bright enough to interfere with stargazing. It gave me an appreciation for why astronomers devote their entire lives to studying the universe. It also gave me an appreciation for why the early, indigenous people of this wilderness would have such a profound belief in a spiritual being.

The human mind is an amazing thing, as all this philosophizing flashed through my head in a matter of seconds, triggered by the simple realization that it was a cloudy morning and we might not be able to sit out tonight and look to the heavens. We'd keep our rain gear handy when we launched the canoes this morning

We all chipped in to prepare the morning meal, which today consisted of pan-fried walleye fillets and peanut butter on bread. A little weird maybe, but nourishing and satisfying, nonetheless. Afterward, we sat and drank our coffee with maps spread across our laps, planning our last few days. Today was Friday, and we had to be back at the ranger station before 3:00 on Sunday afternoon. It gave us two and a half days to get there which, barring catastrophe, should not be a problem.

This morning we had a short paddle to the portage into Darky Lake. We estimated the portage would take at least an hour, maybe more. Then we would head to the southern end of Darky to see the pictographs before heading back to the north end where we'd camp somewhere near the mouth of the Darky River. Of course, we would fish our way through the lake. We'd caught some good fish here when we came through on Monday morning after camping in Wicksteed, so we looked forward to another walleye or trout lunch and dinner.

Then tomorrow we'd head through the Darky River, ending up somewhere in Minn Lake for our final night. Weather permitting, that would give us an easy trip through Minn and back into Lac La Croix to the ranger station well before 3:00. We felt it was a solid plan.

Having finished breakfast, we cleaned our pans and utensils, doused the fire, and drained the last of this morning's coffee. We then packed our gear, made a final inspection of the camp to be sure we were leaving no sign that we'd been there, and loaded the canoes.

Tom offered me the stern again, and I gladly took it. It was fun to steer, and I felt I was getting pretty good at it. Many things that were a mystery to me just a week ago were now part of my daily routine. I'd been immersed for almost a week now in a world I had known very little about. A world that was mysterious and beautiful but could also be angry and dangerous under different conditions.

This morning's conditions were rather benign. It was overcast and humid with just a hint of a breeze. It was quite comfortable, actually. I guessed the temperature to be in the low 70s as we paddled silently around a bend to the right and out into the open water of Brent Lake. We trolled without success while we headed for the portage into Darky Lake. As we got closer, the western shore, which looked flat from a distance, began to define itself a little better. According to our maps, we were looking for a reasonably prominent point, to the left of which should be our landfall for the portage. It's amazing how everything looks the same from the vantage point of a canoe, sitting just 2-3 feet above water level.

Not until we were within a couple of hundred yards, did we see that we were coming up on a pretty flat shoreline. We couldn't quite figure out if the point we were looking for was to our right or to our left. After stopping and looking closely at our maps, we decided we needed to go to the right.

Tom and I took the lead and paddled north, staying about twenty feet off the shoreline, looking for any visible sign of a path or a place where canoes had previously been brought ashore. About a quarter mile up we saw a light spot in the wall of green. As we paddled closer, we noticed a place near a beautiful stand of birches that looked like it had seen some traffic. Pulling ashore, we found a path heading into the interior. There was a definite portage, but it was a lot shorter than it appeared on our maps. The one we were looking for seemed to be at least a quarter mile and this one was only a couple hundred yards long, if that.

After studying the maps some more, we decided that what we were looking at was just a short haul into a long, narrow pond, and the longer portage was at the far end of that pond. We unloaded our gear and made the short round-trip in about ten minutes. We launched again into the pond and paddled to the far end which was only about a quarter mile away. Sure enough, after just a few minutes, there was another obvious take-out. We all agreed that this must be the main portage we were looking for that would take us back into Darky Lake.

Yet again, we unloaded all of the gear and began the trek. We feared this portage could be a long, tough one. On the maps, it appeared to be about a half-mile, maybe more. We just hoped it wouldn't be as severe as the Pond to Gratton portage we'd endured on day 2. Bill and I hefted the canoes to start. I still hadn't mastered the art of getting a canoe from the ground onto my shoulders. Bill and Wayne were bigger and stronger than Tom and I and seemed to handle the initial lift with considerably more ease. Tom, who was a varsity wrestler in high school, could do it, though it was still awkward for him. Try as I might, I still couldn't get the damned thing on my back without some assistance.

Once I got it up and balanced, I could handle it for a while, though it was always a struggle for me. I could manage all the other chores on the trip without a problem but getting that canoe on my shoulders just confounded me to no end. So, off we went, heads down, just plowing forward. After about fifteen minutes, I just had to stop to rest. Tom and Wayne were ahead of us and called back that there was a beautiful waterfall, a great place to take a break. "Thank God!" I said to myself.

A hundred yards up the path, Tom helped unburden me of the canoe, so it didn't fall into a tree and get dented. I could hear the waterfall before I could see it. We grabbed a couple of tin cups from a pack and cautiously stepped down some rocks to where we could reach the river. It really was a beautiful spot, and we held the cups under the falls and drank to our heart's content. Even though it was cloudy, this place seemed magical to me, and I didn't want to leave.

After an adequate rest period, we traded loads and kept plugging onward. It was indeed a long, tough portage with some elevation changes, a few boggy, wet spots and a couple downed trees to circumvent. Overall, with our rest stops, this portage took us nearly two hours to complete. Before we re-launched into Darky Lake, we were all getting hungry. Not wanting to waste a lot of time since the portage had taken so long, we opted for peanut butter sandwiches and Oreos. Besides, we didn't have any fish and were nearly out of most of the other stuff we'd brought. We decided we had to catch some fish for dinner sometime this afternoon while paddling around Darky or we'd risk enduring another meal of peanut butter sandwiches or pancakes tonight.

Before launching, we saw on our maps that we'd have to navigate a long narrows then make our way around several islands, before heading to open water and the south end of Darky where we'd see the pictographs. The other guys had seen these before and they were anxious to show them to me too. Tom said they were pictures of people in canoes and some moose painted on granite walls a few feet above the waterline. They must have been painted from canoes unless the artist was standing on the ice in the winter, which seemed highly unlikely. He said that previous outfitters had told him whoever did the paintings had likely made paint out of ground-up, iron-rich ferrite, probably mixed with fish oil or bear grease which is why all the pictographs are a reddish color. I was really looking forward to seeing them.

It was still gray and overcast as we made our way west. The narrows were still beautiful in the dull gray light, and we saw two deer standing at the shoreline drinking. We also saw loons diving out of sight then resurfacing twenty or thirty feet from where they had disappeared. We all had lines in the water trying to catch our dinner for the evening, but never got a strike through this section.

Once we exited the narrows into the central part of Darky Lake, we headed south, navigating around several islands on our way to the granite walls, trolling all the while. We still hadn't picked up a fish, although Wayne had a hit on his Rapala while rounding a rocky point but couldn't set the hook.

Since it was now around 2:00, we opted to reel in our lines and paddle a little faster. We had a lot of water to cover first getting to the pictographs, then turning around and heading back up to the far north end of the lake, near the mouth of the Darky River where we intended to camp for the night. It was still gray and humid although we hadn't yet had a drop of rain.

About twenty minutes later, Bill pointed to a brighter area in the distance that contrasted to the green wooded shoreline we were used to seeing. Heading that way, the cliffs became evident as we got closer. A few minutes later, we paddled up to the base and could see one pictograph showing several canoes, each shaped like a smile, bearing two crude figures, which looked more like just square heads sticking up from the craft. It also showed a clear picture of a moose. Another showed a large moose with another small moose behind it. Below the head of the large moose was a trail of dots going down. I wondered what that signified. My uneducated guess was that it was water dripping from its chin after raising its head out of the water. Moose are herbivores and eat tender aquatic vegetation in shallows.

After doing some present-day research, it seems that scientists can't quite agree on the age of these paintings, but they are likely at least several hundred years old. The figures I saw were all still quite vivid considering they've been exposed to heat, cold, wind, rain, snow, and sleet for centuries. Visitors are asked never to touch the pictographs, and some feel that they shouldn't be photographed either, out of respect for the people who created them. I felt honored to have been able to see them up so close.

There are many pictograph sites throughout Quetico and the Boundary Waters as well as the entire Canadian Shield for that matter. All appear to have similar themes of canoes and moose. It seemed to me that the moose of this region were as essential to the survival of early residents, as the bison were to the natives of the Great Plains. Seeing these pictographs had a sobering effect on me. Tom said that they'd all felt the same way every time they'd seen them. Our voices fell naturally into a hush while in their presence.

It was now coming up on 3:00 and we still had quite a lot of water to cover and some fish to catch. We paddled silently away from the cliffs, and our voices inexplicably became a little louder the further away we traveled. I reflected on that later. It wasn't a conscious decision to speak softly in the presence of the pictographs. It was very much like the feeling you get walking through a cemetery. We all seem to lower our voices out of respect for the dead.

We were probably a quarter of a mile away, heading north before we all got our fishing gear back out and lines back into the water. We needed to do some serious fishing before evening, or we'd be forced to eat peanut butter again. That was not a comforting thought.

As we paddled back into open water, we looked ahead for islands and rocky shoals which would be more likely to hold fish. We steered towards them while keeping to a generally northern tack. It was still gray but not raining, perfect fishing conditions from my experience, as fish were more likely to be shallower and more active than in bright sunlight which often drives them deep.

We passed a rocky shoal with just a little bit of rock showing above the surface, very much like the one that Tom and I had found in Conmee two days ago. Paddling close by, we could see extensive rock formations below the surface, and decided to cast the outer edges, all the way around. The wind was barely a factor, so it was easy to maneuver the canoes. As we got around to the north side of the shoal, Tom hooked a fish. I reeled in my line and grabbed the net as I watched him play it. The fish fought deep then went under the canoe to the other side as Tom followed with his rod tip. He got it to the surface, and I slipped the net under a nice walleye. Dinner!

Wayne then hooked another one about 200 feet away around on the west side of the shoal, and as Bill was reeling in his line to get it out of the way, he hooked one too! This was the first "double-header" of our trip, when one canoe had two fish on at the same time. I watched as Bill held his rod in one hand and netted Wayne's fish with the other. Wayne then unhooked his fish and took the now-empty net and deftly scooped up Bill's fish. After almost no action all day long, we suddenly had three good fish in a matter of five minutes. This shoal was a fish magnet!

It was coming up on 4:30 and we had more than enough to feed us for dinner tonight, plus breakfast tomorrow. We considered sticking around to just fish for sport a while longer but ultimately decided to pack it in and head up to the north end to try and find a good campsite for the night. It was still overcast but getting a little brighter in the west. We hoped the skies would clear enough to see a sunset and maybe get another night of stargazing. The breeze was gentle, and the lake was calm as we paddled unhurriedly through the open water towards the north shore of Darky Lake.

About 20 minutes later, we closed in on a good-sized island in the north end, just west of the mouth of the Darky River. We'd seen this island on Monday morning as we passed through after our night of camping in Wicksteed. From the water, it looked as promising then, as it did now so we pulled ashore to look around before unloading. It had all the attributes we desired, including a level place to pitch the tent, a good-sized fire pit, places to sit, and the all-important sky-viewing rock. We unloaded our gear and set about making it home for the night.

I started filleting our catch while Wayne and Tom went inland in search of firewood and Bill began pitching the tent. The elusive, yet somehow ever-present gulls magically appeared en masse to fight over the carcasses of the walleyes I'd cleaned. Once they'd settled all their disputes over who got what, they disappeared to wherever they go when they're not eating fish guts. It's still a mystery to me. I put the fillets in a pot of water and covered them to prevent gull-theft and started unpacking the cooking gear.

Wayne and Tom walked back into camp with a couple of armloads of dry firewood. Quetico regulations required campers to use only sticks, branches, and logs that had already fallen.

Cutting of live trees or branches was prohibited. It seemed we never really had any difficulty finding suitable firewood as nature has a way of continuously trimming deadwood through wind, ice, and snow.

We soon got a good fire going, started melting some butter in the pan, and rolled four beautiful walleye fillets in flour. Bill said we were down to our last two potatoes and asked if we should save one for tomorrow. "Hell no!" Tom piped up, and we all concurred. Bill got out his trusty fillet knife and surgically prepared the thinnest sliced potatoes we'd had this whole trip. He kept the skins on so there was no waste.

I must say at this point that Bill was our master campfire chef. I'd found out over the last 6 days that there's a real art to getting the fire and coals just right. It also matters how close to the coals you place the pan to get an even heat which prevents burning while also getting the fare fully cooked to just a nice golden brown. I told him, "People should hire you to be their camp cook!" to which he replied, "It wouldn't be any fun if I *had* to do it."

It made me wonder if wilderness guides thought of their jobs as work or if it was a joyful pursuit. It would probably depend a lot on the personalities of your clients. It would surely be a long week if they were jerks who thought they "knew it all!" On the other hand, it could be very rewarding with a group of fun people who appreciated seeing, feeling, and learning about this wild and wonderful place.

It was still cloudy, but warm as we sat around after dinner. We decided to go for a swim, as the campsite had a terrific built-in swimming hole just off the little canoe take-out. After a refreshing swim, we got into dry clothes and hung our newly washed ones on some tree limbs to dry overnight. We couldn't string a clothesline because we were using our rope to hang the food packs out of reach of bears. We still had not seen a bear but had seen signs of their presence and didn't want to take any chances.

It was still dry but overcast, so we there would be no sunset or stargazing on this night. We sat around the campfire, poking it every so often, sending a flurry of orange sparks into the night, as we re-lived the day. Oddly enough, we discovered a collective craving for Pepsi on ice. The tranquility finally got the better of us and, as the fire died, we headed for the tent.

This would be our next to last night in Quetico. I had mixed feelings as I climbed into my sleeping bag. I was missing my family but was also excited to travel the Darky River tomorrow as we headed into Minn Lake. From all we'd heard from our outfitter, the fishing was terrific in the Darky. That was my last thought as I drifted off to sleep.

Day 7

I awoke early Saturday morning to the steady pitter-patter of light rain hitting the tent. There was no thunder or lightning, nor was there any wind to speak of. Not being a morning person, I merely took this as an excuse to sleep in a while longer. I didn't know what time it was, but there was barely any light, and I saw no purpose in getting out of my warm, dry sleeping bag. I heard some commotion, and then Wayne said, "I gotta take a leak," so out he went and off into the woods. Tom just turned over without a word, and soon, I could hear him snoring softly. Bill hadn't even stirred.

I laid there with my eyes closed, listening to the gentle rain, thinking about the day to come. It would be our last full day in Quetico, and I had mixed emotions. I was beginning to look forward to civilization again but was still excited about the prospects for *this* day, paddling through the Darky River. I hoped the rain would stop, or at least not get any heavier. We'd been lucky so far. Apart from Wednesday in Conmee, we'd had spectacular weather, so we really had little to complain about.

I heard Wayne's footsteps in the distance, then getting closer and wondered if he'd get back in the tent and try to go back to sleep. Shortly, I heard him rustling through his pack, no doubt looking for his rain gear.

At least we'd had the presence of mind to cover our backpacks with the tarp last night before heading for the tent. I laid there quietly for several more minutes trying to decipher what Wayne was doing. He was walking around, then rustling through his pack again, then walking away towards the fire pit, then back again. I finally couldn't stand the suspense anymore and poked my head out and asked, "What's up?", "It's raining," he said, to which I replied, "No shit?" He said he was looking for some dry matches to try to get a fire going.

By this time, I was wide awake and had little hope of getting in a few more winks. I decided to get up and give him a hand. I rummaged through my own pack and put on my rain pants and a rain jacket. We found some dry matches in a plastic bag in the cooking pack and found some twigs and small sticks that had stayed dry under the tarp. We had something to work with, but we'd need some bigger stuff to get a decent fire going in the rain. I headed into the woods to look for some bigger sticks and found several that had stayed relatively dry under a blow-down. I also split a few small logs with the camp ax to get at the inner sapwood.

Carefully arranging our kindling around a few pinecones with slightly bigger wood on top, I struck a match. Within five minutes we had a pretty good little fire going. I took the coffee pot down to the lake and filled it with water.

Tom and Bill were still sleeping, so Wayne and I sat by the fire with our coffee mugs and chatted about today's trip through the Darky River. He said that after last year's trip, one of the guys at the outfitter suggested they do the Darky next time because the fishing was excellent, and the portages were relatively easy. Besides, clients reported moose sightings along the Darky every year. We were running out of time to see a moose and had high hopes we'd get to see one today.

The rain was very light and really didn't pose a big problem. It wasn't a cold rain, so we didn't have to bundle up. We just needed to protect our packs because they held the only dry clothes we had left. The ones we "washed" during last evening's swim were still hanging on the trees where we'd left them last night and were obviously wetter than when we'd hung them up.

Hearing some rustling coming from the tent, Tom poked his head out and said, "Hey, it's raining." Simultaneously, Wayne and I said, "No shit?" Tom exited the tent and after quickly finding his rain gear, joined us by the fire. He poured some Folger's freeze-dried instant coffee crystals into his mug, followed by hot water from the coffeepot and joined the discussion. He said we had all day to navigate and fish the Darky. All we had to do was get to Minn Lake in time to set up camp by tonight. We'd have no trouble getting to the ranger station by 3:00 tomorrow from anywhere in Minn. He also hoped we might see a moose today. "For sure we'll see some beaver dams and hopefully a beaver," he added.

Bill was now stirring and poked his head out. Thankfully, he didn't state the obvious, he just grunted, stood up and yawned loudly. He put on his rain gear and joined the breakfast club around the fire. We still had some leftover walleye fillets from yesterday as well as some pancake mix and syrup, so after draining a cup of coffee, Bill got to it. Walleye and pancakes! I wondered how I'd handle a boring breakfast of cereal and toast when I got home.

After breakfast, we cleaned the pans and dishes, broke down the tent, loaded the packs, doused the fire, and threw our wet clothes from yesterday into the bottom of the canoes. There was no way we'd get them dry before we left Quetico and saw little use in trying. With a light rain falling, we loaded the canoes and headed for the mouth of the Darky River, full of expectations. Up to now, we'd only flirted with short rivers here and there, but today we'd spend the entire day on a river. I thought that was going to be an exciting way to spend our last full day here.

Had it not been raining, the surface of the lake would have been like glass. As it was, the calm surface was dappled with millions of little circles as the raindrops found their new home. It was beautiful in its own way.

As we entered the river, we began to fish by casting rather than by trolling. As we got further into the river, and it began to narrow, we could cast from the middle to both banks. Tom got the first hit on his shallow running Rapala, a beautiful smallmouth that put on quite an exhibition, making several runs with acrobatic jumps in-between. When he got it to the side of the canoe, I reached over and grabbed it by the lower lip and hauled it aboard. I handed it to Tom, and he held it up for Wayne and Bill to see. After admiring it for a few seconds, he eased it back into the river where it quickly disappeared.

Being in the river rather than out in the open lakes had a very different feel about it, much more intimate and immediate. We were constantly scanning both banks, looking for wildlife. The lead canoe was also looking ahead for obstacles like rocks, tree limbs, blowdowns, and anything else that could present a hazard to our navigation and cause us to capsize or get hung-up.

It was an exciting change of pace and kept us on our toes. The fishing too was totally different.

Out in the main parts of the lakes, we could easily troll without the concern of getting hung up on underwater obstacles. In the river, we had to "target" cast to openings, sometimes getting a lure snagged on a submerged log or branch. This would generally mean paddling over to the obstacle and reeling the rod tip all the way down to the snagged lure and trying to jerk it back and forth in order to free it up. More than once, we had to break it off and tie on a new lure.

We caught fish nearly everywhere. Mostly smallmouth bass, but also quite a few northern pike in the 4-5-pound range. This was a fishing paradise! We completely ignored the light rain as we were having way too much fun. About an hour into the river, it widened, and there was a small island. This was a beautiful place, even on a cloudy, rainy day. We were fortunate to see several eagles perched high above in white pines and saw another one cruising up the river just below treetop level. We also observed numerous deer and muskrats.

Once we passed the island, the river narrowed again, and we came to our first portage of the day. We were ready to stretch our legs, and this was a gorgeous place to do it. There was a small waterfall we had to go around, and we pulled the canoes up onto the bank and unloaded our gear before exploring a little bit.

This portage showed on our map as being relatively short, maybe an eighth of a mile or a little more. The take-out was a bit small for two canoes and a pile of gear, but otherwise, it was a pretty easy portage compared to some we'd dealt with earlier in the week. Tom and Wayne hefted the canoes for this one. Bill and I led the way with the packs, and when we got to the north end, there was a terrific looking pool, below the falls, that we thought would hold some fish. We dropped the packs, then helped Tom and Wayne rid themselves of the canoes. After lingering a few minutes to catch our breath, we headed back to retrieve the rest of the packs and the fishing gear.

When we returned, we made some casts from shore to see if we could scare up a fish or two from the pool, but to no avail. There were a couple of blowdowns that hindered our ability to cast to places we wanted, so we loaded up again and launched. Once we were back in the canoes, we could fish the pool without restrictions, and Bill caught a big pike right off the bat. This one was around three feet long and must have weighed about ten pounds. After he released it, we headed north again, casting as we went while scouring the banks for wildlife. We quietly drifted with the gentle current and spoke softly. It seemed an intrusion to make any noise at all. The rain had slowed to a light drizzle.

Out of the corner of my eye, I caught some movement ahead near the left bank. Whatever it was didn't show itself again for several long moments then surfaced again. It was brown and sleek and a great swimmer, disappearing again around some tree roots that extended into the river. As we came nearer, we were all watching as it re-surfaced about twenty feet away. I recognized it as a river otter, fishing for its breakfast over, under, and around the roots where smaller fish might hide. It saw us and then disappeared with a splash. I loved seeing these creatures in their own environment, living their lives as God intended.

I was content to leave my fishing rod laying across the gunwale and just immerse myself in the natural world around me, looking for movement, listening to the birds, and the water as it made its way with a gurgle around rocks and trees that had blown over into the path of the current. Moving water has a very different sound and feel to it. The slow current carried us silently forward without much work on our part except for an occasional paddle thrust to keep us facing forward.

After another mile, we came upon some mild, shallow rapids. At the top end, it wasn't deep enough to float the canoe, so we stepped out into the gravelly riverbed and walked it to where the water was a little deeper and swift enough to carry us down to the pool below. I stepped back into the canoe and off we went, running our first rapids of the trip. This was fun!

As we got to the pool, about a hundred yards downstream, I was laughing and said to Tom, "Wow, that was great!" I got no reply and turned around to see that Tom wasn't in the canoe. Looking back upstream, I saw him standing at the top of the rapids with his hands on his hips staring down at me. I assumed he had gotten back in when I did. Sheepishly, I paddled over to the left bank and waited while he waded down to meet me and said sarcastically, "Thanks for waiting for me to get in." Bill and Wayne shot the little rapids together and met up with us. We all had a good laugh, then continued for another half-mile to our second portage of the day.

This one wasn't very long but went uphill at first, which was tough, especially since I had volunteered my well-honed canoe-carrying services. As usual, I had to have Tom's help to get the beast over my head and balanced on my shoulders. Bill took the other canoe while Tom and Wayne led the way, carrying backpacks. The first fifty yards or so were brutally steep before cresting and heading gently downhill the rest of the way. Although I was in better shape than I was a week ago, Bill conceded that this was a tough climb, which made me feel a little better about it. It only took about fifteen minutes to reach the other end. On the way back to get the rest of the gear, we stopped and admired the beautiful little waterfall that was the reason for the portage.

Once we'd gotten everything to the put-in side, we stopped for a snack of peanut butter sandwiches and Oreos. We had about a half-package of Oreos left, which was enough to last one more day. These guys knew from past trips that peanut butter sandwiches and Oreos can sustain life for a long time, so they always packed plenty of both.

After our lunch break, we loaded up and headed out again, feeling refreshed and strong. The drizzle was persistent, but not bothersome since nearly everything we had was already wet anyway. This part of the Darky was very serene, with tall spruce, tamarack, cedar, and pine forest lining the banks. There were many places with little shallow coves that looked like the perfect backdrop for a moose sighting, but there were none to be seen. We had, however been lucky enough to see at least a dozen deer. Some were drinking from the river, while others, startled by our sudden appearance, took off running through the woods with their white flag tails signaling the alarm to others as they fled. I was still fully invested in the beauty of Quetico, not taking any of this for granted.

We continued to follow the river north and then around a big bend to the west where we saw a beaver dam blocking a small creek that fed into the river. As we got closer, we heard a loud "smack" as one of them warned of our approach. We didn't get to see the beaver, but I really admired the engineering skills of these common Quetico residents. Their homes required constant maintenance, packing a little mud here and another branch there to keep the water level up on the pond side and keep their home dry on the inside. The entrance to their domed abode was underwater to protect them and their young from predators.

The river got a little wider as it turned to the west, and we sporadically caught fish throughout, mostly smallmouth bass and northern pike with an occasional walleye. We needed to start planning our dinner for camp tonight in Minn Lake. We still had a portage or two to go before reaching Minn and didn't want to have to carry a stringer of fish with us, so we released everything we caught in the river.

About mid-afternoon, the drizzle finally stopped, and the sky got brighter, but the sun still hadn't made an appearance. We shed our rain gear and were much more comfortable.

About a half-hour later, we reached the next portage which appeared on our map to be a little longer than the others we had today. As we approached, we heard what sounded like a falls or rapids. It turned out to be a series of rapids that were too shallow and long to run or even pull the canoes through. There was a distinct take-out on the south bank, so we beached the canoes and had a reasonably flat but mucky hike for several hundred yards to a point below the rapids. It was easy except for the mud.

According to our maps, we had about another mile or so to reach Minn Lake. We were uncertain if we had any more portages, but the map showed the river had a "pinch-point" between us and Minn that might be rapids. It would be fun if it were a mild one that we could run. Tom reminded me that he had missed the only one we'd had so far when I left him behind. About twenty minutes later we came up to the pinch-point and saw it was, in fact, a rapids, but was too shallow to run. We ended up having to get out and drag the canoes so, thanks to me, Tom had missed his only opportunity to run a rapids.

When we got to the bottom, we could see ahead that the river opened into what we assumed was Minn

Lake, which was where we would need to find a campsite for our last night in Quetico. We broke out the fishing gear and prepared to begin trolling again, hoping to catch a few walleyes for our "last supper."

By now it was around 4:00 and we elected to troll for another hour before stopping for the night. There were a lot of islands in Minn Lake, so we figured it shouldn't be too difficult to find a suitable site. Besides, we needed to catch some fish for dinner.

It was still overcast, but it wasn't raining. Leaving the Darky River behind left me feeling a little sad. It felt like the trip was over, even though we had another night and most of tomorrow before boarding our floatplane back to the real world.

My reverie was broken when I heard Wayne call out "fish on!" We stopped paddling, reeled in our lines, and watched as his rod bent towards the water as the fish went deep. Bill was in the stern, working his paddle to help Wayne keep the fish in front of him. It was fighting deep, barely giving an inch as Wayne adjusted his drag and fought to keep it from breaking his line. On they went, fish vs. man, for another ten minutes or so before the fish tired enough for Wayne to get it to the surface. It was another mammoth Laker of at least ten pounds, maybe more. After Bill netted the big fish, Wayne held it up for pictures, gave it a kiss, and gently released it. It wallowed near the surface for about thirty seconds, then recovered enough to slowly disappear straight down into the depths of Minn Lake. That was as much fun for us to watch as it probably was for Wayne to catch. That fish earned its freedom.

We still didn't have any fish for dinner tonight, so we began trolling our way to the south, towards the shoreline and a series of islands that appeared on the map. We crossed about a half-mile of open water before arriving near the first of several islands. We didn't get any strikes in the open water and began paddling around the first of the islands, looking for fish as well as looking for a suitable campsite.

As we headed around a point, we saw three smaller islands behind this bigger one. None of them seemed to have a campsite on them, but as we went around the west side of the smallest island, Wayne had a hit on a deep running Rapala. After a brief battle, Bill slipped the net under a small walleye. It was only about 12" long, so we let it go, but felt this area might hold more, so we began to cast. After several fruitless casts, I hooked a fish that seemed bigger than the one we'd just released. It fought deep for a minute, then slowly came to the surface. Sure enough, it was another walleye, this one about 16", weighing at least two pounds, maybe more. We put it on a stringer and kept casting. If we could get one or two more fish like this one, we'd have enough for dinner tonight and breakfast tomorrow. I had just put this fish on the stringer when Tom caught another one just like it. This was a honey hole! We stayed there for another half hour just catching fish after fish, releasing all but three. There appeared to be a pretty big school of walleyes hanging off this point. They were all in the one to two pound plus range, not huge, but great fun to catch and perfect size for eating

.

With the fishing action slowing down, we put away the rods and began a serious search for a good campsite. According to our map, there was a pretty good-sized island another half-mile to the southwest, so we headed that way through another stretch of open water. It was still cloudy, but without wind or rain, and the temperature was still comfortable.

The lake was calm, and the distant shoreline began to take shape as we drew closer. To our right was an island with a narrows between it and the left shore. We paddled into the slot and examined both banks for any sign of a campsite. Finding nothing, we continued around the island to the right and found a take-out on the southern shore. There was a narrow little sandy beach and a path leading up to a flatter area. It was big enough for one tent, and it had a rather small fire pit. The only thing lacking was an unobstructed view of the sky from the campsite. We were still hoping for a last night of stargazing, but the overcast didn't seem to have any breaks in it, so it was doubtful we'd have a clear sky anyway.

Bill put up a weak argument for finding another site "just in case," but the rest of us overruled him. We decided to stay here and set up our last camp. It was a little more cramped than any of the others we'd used, but we were a small party, and it would do just fine. There was no guarantee that we'd find anything better if we kept looking.

We all pitched in again, I cleaned the fish and offered the fish guts and bones to the scavengers, who appeared again as if they'd followed us all day, waiting to pounce. Wayne set up the tent, Tom gathered firewood, and Bill got out the cooking gear. Within forty-five minutes of setting foot on this island, we had walleye fillets in the frying pan and spaghetti in a pot of boiling water. We were all famished, having had nothing but a peanut butter sandwich and some Oreos since breakfast.

While the meal cooked, Tom again lamented that he craved a Pepsi on ice. We all then joined in, discussing what we were going to have tomorrow night when we arrived back in Ely. A Pepsi was very high on everyone's list as were cheeseburgers. Nobody mentioned fish or spaghetti. It had been a few days since we had any bacon or eggs, so that was sounding good again too. Bill wanted a big steak. We decided we'd look for a different restaurant than the log cabin café we had eaten in twice before we left.

Bill announced that dinner was served, and we all held out our tin plates. He rewarded us each with two fillets and a forkful of spaghetti. We still had four more fillets for breakfast tomorrow. The discussion continued over dinner, but digressed to travel plans, family, work, and back again to what a wonderful trip we'd had so far. The maps showed we had one more portage tomorrow between Minn and Lac La Croix.

After eating, we cleaned up our messes and put some water on to boil for coffee and hot chocolate. There was no sign of a break in the clouds, so we resigned ourselves that we had done the last of our stargazing. It was getting dark as we sat around the fire, talking about our favorite parts of the trip. My comrades had done this many times before, so of course they had different impressions than I did. I enjoyed nearly everything and had trouble picking out just a few moments.

I loved the overall majesty of this big wilderness, but also recalled the little things I had seen like the way the ancient cedars sent their roots looking for footholds among the granite boulders, and the sounds of the loons and watching chipmunks scurrying around the forest floor looking for seeds or pine nuts. We all marveled at the burnt island and lamented not seeing a moose. There was still tomorrow, but the chances of seeing one now seemed very slim. We loved seeing the river otter, and my buddies said that we saw more eagles on this trip than they ever had before. The fishing had been terrific nearly everywhere we went.

When Tom asked what I didn't like, I could only come up with two things. The first was the portage from Pond Lake to Gratton, and the other was the windy crossing in Conmee. I confessed that I was scared shitless, both ways! They all admitted that it was a tough day. They also said they'd never do the Pond-Gratton portage again. As the conversation waned, the fire died to orange embers, and we retired to the tent for the last time.

Day 8

The birds were the first ones up this morning. I heard them chirping in the trees outside the tent and laid there for a few minutes getting my brain in gear. No one else was stirring and I took the quiet time to contemplate the day, the past week, and the week to come. Part of me hated to see this week come to an end, but the other part was anxious to see Mary Jane and the kids. I had a job waiting with tasks piling up in my absence. I pushed that thought from my mind because I didn't want it to tarnish this final day in Quetico. I wanted to embrace it.

It was still pretty dark, with just a bare hint of light showing through the walls of the tent. I looked at my watch. I could barely make it out to be about 5:45, so not quite sunrise. I wanted to peek out to see if it was still cloudy but didn't want to disturb my tent mates. Making a vain attempt to go back to sleep, my mind was now much too busy. I decided I had to pee, and once that thought entered my mind, I could think of little else. I slowly exited my sleeping bag and tried desperately to sneak out of the tent without waking anyone else, and promptly tripped over the nylon flap and fell in a heap outside the tent.

Someone stirred as I reached back inside to grab my shoes so I could go off and take care of my business. I walked quietly into the woods. I looked up and it was still so dark it was hard to tell if was clear or cloudy. Since there was no dew clinging to the branches, I assumed it was cloudy but silently hoped we'd have a bright, sunny, final day in this wilderness paradise.

Having completed my task, I tried to sneak back into camp without disturbing anyone. Tom was poking his head out of the tent as I approached and asked, "What kind of day are we gonna have?"

I said, "I think it's still cloudy, but I don't feel any rain. There's no dew on anything." Tom exited the tent, a little more gracefully than I had. He tousled his hair, rubbed his eyes, stretched and finished his ritual with a loud yawn before heading out in the direction from which I'd just returned.

Hearing more rustling coming from the tent, I assumed Wayne and Bill were coming to life. I began putting together the makings of a fire with some pinecones, twigs and small branches. I had a couple of larger branches ready to add as needed and struck a match. The sap from the pinecones caught and then spread to the twigs. I heard little snaps as the fire took hold and the flames grew, warding off the morning chill. Once the fire was established, I took the coffee pot and filled it with the clear, pure water from Minn

Lake then set up a little rock stand and set the pot to heat.

Everyone was now up and waiting for the water to heat so we could have our morning coffee. Bill declared that breakfast would consist of the last of our walleye fillets along with pancakes, since that's pretty much all we had left, besides a half-package of Oreos and some peanut butter. Having done this so many times before, they had planned our provisions well.

Once the water was hot, we passed the Folgers around, and Tom went from cup to cup adding the hot water that magically turned the odd little freeze-dried crystals into coffee. I had gotten accustomed to instant coffee over the last week or so, but still craved the "real stuff" from home. As we sat, we discussed the plans for our last day. According to the map, we were only a couple of miles from the ranger station but had one more portage to negotiate between Minn and Lac la Croix. Even so, we had plenty of time to get there before 3:00.

We took our time with breakfast this morning, enjoying the casual feel of our last meal in the wilds of the Quetico wilderness. We would fish only for sport today as our mindsets were quickly changing from solitude to civilization. We bemoaned the fact that we hadn't seen a moose, but also were mildly astonished that we hadn't seen even one other person in the last eight days. It's a testament to how wild and remote this park is and how well-managed in terms of permits allowed. There are not many places on earth that are as accessible to the average person, yet still as wild, serene, and unspoiled as Quetico Provincial Park and the Boundary Waters Canoe Area.

As we cleaned up our dishes, pots, and pans, and broke down the tent, then loaded our packs for the last time, it began to rain lightly. Our hopes for a sunny last day had been dashed. Our clothes from a couple of days ago were still wet and we were now wearing our last dry ones. We got our rain gear out of the packs, suited up, and gave the campsite one last inspection to erase any remaining sign that we'd been here. It was already after 9:00. We'd been lazy this morning, reluctant to leave because it signaled the end of our adventure.

Apparently, I had earned Tom's trust as a helmsman as he jumped into the bow without explanation and handed me his paddle. I felt like a seasoned veteran, and steering a canoe felt as natural to me as driving a car. We launched into the rain-dappled waters of Minn Lake and broke out our fishing rods right away to begin trolling. As we headed south from our campsite, it still felt wild and remote, even though we were only a couple of miles from our entry point. We dallied about, paddling around the island, wasting time because we'd rather spend it here than sitting around at the ranger station.

Wayne got a fish on almost immediately, fighting a smallmouth bass that jumped three or four times before submitting to the net. It was only about a pound and a half but put up a fight like a much bigger fish. The fish we'd caught over the last week or so were all very healthy looking and strong. They were scrappy fighters; their colors were good, and they reflected the good health of their environment.

We stayed near the northwest shoreline as we proceeded slowly to the southwest towards our next, and final, portage. We all picked up fish here and there, mostly smallmouth bass but Tom caught a northern pike and Wayne caught a couple of walleyes that we would have kept had we been planning another meal. Knowing we had only hours left, we felt like the trip was essentially over, and our hearts weren't in it anymore. It was a rather odd, melancholy feeling and we were just going through the motions as we came up to the last portage. I wanted one more crack at getting a canoe on my shoulders without assistance. It was a matter of personal pride.

This portage was only about an eighth of a mile long and appeared to be relatively flat and a little wider than most we had encountered. After we pulled the canoes up on the bank, we sat in the light rain and had peanut butter fold-over sandwiches. I told the guys I was going to get that damned canoe over my head and onto my shoulders by myself or I was going to die trying! They all laughed and said, "Go for it!"

After finishing our snack, I prepared myself. I emptied the contents of the canoe and stared it down. It just sat there mocking me, daring me to pick it up. I steeled myself, took a deep breath, grabbed the crossbar, and yelled out as I hefted it over my head and onto my shoulders. I stumbled a little, then regained my balance and let out a loud whoop in exaltation! Off I went down the path of righteous victory toward the put-in at Lac La Croix. I had finally done it... on the last day! It felt great. Due to the last couple of days of rain, the path was a mucky mess of mud and moose grass, but I was oblivious to it. I had finally conquered my last remaining demon of this trip.

When we got to the end, I put the load down like a pro, then raised my arms to the sky like Rocky Balboa. Wayne was carrying the other canoe and followed my lead. Tom and Bill were already waiting for us and applauded our performance. We rested a few minutes, then went back for the other four backpacks and our fishing rods. We now had nothing between us and the ranger station but a mile or so of water and islands. It was about 1:30 and we could have made the trip in twenty minutes if need be. We slowed our pace, trolling again as we paddled slowly in the rain, trying to postpone the inevitable end of our journey. I caught one more fish and Bill caught two as we navigated the last mile.

We pulled our canoes up to the dock at the ranger station and had a bittersweet moment of reflection as we looked out at the rain-dappled surface of Lac La Croix, where we'd begun this journey a week ago today. There was no floatplane at the dock yet, so we piled our gear and then Tom and Wayne paddled the two canoes over to the little beach and pulled them ashore. We all walked into the ranger station where we checked in and asked about the incoming flight. The ranger on duty told us our ride should be here within the hour and asked if we'd had a good time. We affirmed that we'd had a GREAT time and said we hadn't seen another human or canoe all week.

We chatted with him about our experiences and he was gracious about our enthusiasm. I'm sure he heard the same stories day after day, but he talked to us as if it was all news to him. We'd lost track of the time until we heard the deep rumble of a big radial engine approaching. We went outside to see a big, yellow, DeHavilland Otter touching down on the lake a hundred yards or so offshore. It turned and taxied slowly to the dock, where the ranger helped tie it down. The pilot emerged and we saw it wasn't Dusty.

If the DeHavilland Beaver is a taxi, the Otter is a bus. This plane was empty but could easily hold eight or ten passengers in addition to a crew of two. We were the only party departing here today so we would have our choice of seating. The pilot and co-pilot began loading our gear into the baggage compartment, which was enormous in comparison to that of the Beaver we had arrived in a week ago. The two-man crew was all business and welcomed us aboard, telling us we could sit anywhere we liked. The cabin seemed huge as we found seats and strapped ourselves in for the short flight back to Ely.

After the ranger pushed us off, the pilot called "clear" out his small window and hit the starter. As in the Beaver, the big Pratt & Whitney radial engine belched a puff of white smoke and the engine settled into a satisfying rumble while we taxied slowly away from the dock. It was still raining and there was a solid, gray overcast above the low hanging, scuddy, rain clouds.

Again, there was no appreciable wind, so we took off to the east. Soon after we were airborne, we were flying in and out of the low clouds, getting brief glimpses of the water and islands below. I simply stared out the window, marveling at the watery maze below that looked so different from the air than from a canoe. I was in a bit of a trance when I detected a subtle change in the throttle setting and we began to slowly descend through the rain. A few minutes later, we touched down gently and taxied toward the dock at the Ely seaplane anchorage. We didn't get our pilot's name, but he was every bit as skilled as Dusty was, coasting to a flawless little bump at the dock after shutting down the engine. A dock hand grabbed a rope and tied us down while the pilot opened his door and gracefully stepped down from his perch onto the left float. He opened our door and helped us down the 2-3 steps, then opened the baggage compartment and began piling our wet gear onto the dock.

I suddenly remembered the threat of the Air Traffic Controllers strike and asked him if they had gone out. He said they had, and the ATC system was working at reduced capacity because it was being staffed by supervisors. President Reagan had kept his word and fired every one of the 12,000 or so controllers. I wondered if it would affect my return flight for tomorrow afternoon. My plane was supposed to leave Duluth at 1:20. It was a bit worrisome.

Since we were re-entering the United States, we were met by a customs agent who checked us in and asked if we were bringing anything back into the country from Canada. We told him we weren't bringing any fish or artifacts, just some very nice memories. He accepted our answer and allowed us back into the good old USA using only our driver's licenses for ID.

Wayne started fumbling around in his pack trying to find his car keys so he could open it up and we could load our gear. Everything we had was soaked, but it was just a short ride to the motel we had booked for tonight. It was the same one we'd stayed in before we left a week ago. They had a washer and dryer available and we intended to use it! After a frantic couple of minutes, Wayne came up with his keys and we hauled everything to his car and stuffed it into every nook and cranny we could find.

We planned to take it all to the motel, haul it to our rooms, and sort it out. We'd have to return the cookware and utensils, along with the rented backpacks, to the outfitter in the morning. When we arrived at the motel and got everything safely into our rooms, we each picked out some underwear and shorts and a sweatshirt to immediately load into the motel dryer. None of us had any dry clothes, everything we owned was wet. We flipped coins to see who got to take hot showers first. Tom and I were sharing a room, and Tom won our flip, Wayne won the other one. Bill and I took the wet clothes, wrung them out the best we could, and threw them into the motel dryer right away, feeding it as many dimes as it would take. It wasn't cold out but being wet all day had finally chilled us.

While Tom showered, I called home to tell Mary Jane that I was literally "out of the woods" and that we'd had a fantastic time. She gave me a brief rundown on the happenings at home and that she and the boys were fine and anxious to see me and hear all about the trip. I told her if my flight wasn't canceled that I'd be home tomorrow afternoon and that I'd call her again from the Duluth airport in the morning. After we hung up, I went to the office to see if I could find a newspaper and read about the PATCO strike.

The desk clerk found the remnants of today's Sunday Duluth Tribune and gave it to me. I took it back to the room and scoured it for some news of the strike. We'd been completely out of touch for the last eight days and wouldn't have known if we were at war or an earthquake had leveled San Francisco. The paper revealed that none of that had happened but confirmed that the PATCO strike was now in its third day and the air traffic control system was crippled but not dead. Supervisors were running the system at reduced capacity. The largest markets were hardest hit with reduced numbers of flights. I hoped that Duluth to Lansing would be flying tomorrow!

Tom emerged, wearing a dry towel and said the shower was fantastic! I told him that Bill and I had thrown some clothes in the dryer and we'd soon have some dry clothes to wear. It was now my turn and I could hardly wait to get in the hot shower. I hadn't shaved in more than a week and contemplated not shaving until I got home. Having never grown a beard for more than a few days, I thought I might show it off to Mary Jane, but I didn't know if I could stand it another day. The itching was driving me nuts.

First things first, I hopped into the shower, turned up the heat and just reveled in it. Swimming in the lakes and taking a good hot shower are worlds apart. I was ready for civilization again... give me the shower! I grabbed my razor and without a second thought began removing eight days' worth of facial hair. I couldn't believe how good it felt to be clean-shaven again. Tom was right, it WAS fantastic!

When I emerged, Tom had the paper spread out on one of the beds and was catching up on sports. Larry Nelson was leading the PGA Championship by four shots after three rounds at the Atlanta Athletic Club and the major league baseball strike was over and play was resuming today. We tried unsuccessfully to get the final round of the PGA golf tournament on TV. Ely was a long way from the closest station in Duluth and the rabbit ear antenna was useless. Tom and I had worked together on a golf course ground crew in high school and during college summers. Back then we played at least nine holes together nearly every day after work, so we both had a keen interest in the sport.

Bill rapped on our door and when I opened it, he threw some warm clothes at us, fresh from the dryer. We jumped into the warm, dry clothes and suddenly felt human again. Beginning to sort out the stuff we needed to return to the outfitter in the morning, Tom and I made another pile of wet stuff that still needed to go to the dryer. Bill and Wayne were doing the same.

By now it was nearing 6:00pm, and we were all ready for something different to eat. Walleye is wonderful, but we were ready for some red meat. We looked in the phone book for restaurants. There wasn't a big selection, but we found one that advertised steaks. Bill was determined to have a steak, even if it was a bad steak. We took another load of wet clothes to the dryer and then headed out for dinner. We were back into another life now, one familiar and comfortable. It was as if we'd lived in two entirely different worlds in the same day, which I suppose we had.

We found the restaurant and pulled into a surprisingly crowded parking lot, considering we were in Ely, Minnesota on a Sunday evening. The restaurant was casual but still a step above the log cabin café we'd dined at the night before heading out into the backcountry. We were seated by the hostess at an interior booth with subdued lighting. Our waitress appeared shortly with ice water and menus and asked if we'd like something to drink. We all ordered Pepsi... on ice! She looked at us kind of funny but shrugged and left. When she returned with our Pepsi's, we confused her even more by then ordering a round of Grain Belt Premium in a bottle. The Pepsi was the first drink other than lake water that we'd had in more than a week and tasted great. We downed them before she could return with the beers.

Finally feeling clean and relaxed, our first round of beers started us talking about the trip we'd just completed. The more we drank the more talkative we became, joking about funny things that happened, and lies about fish we'd caught. They all started poking good-natured fun at me and my feeble canoe carrying abilities while praising my filleting prowess.

After a couple of beers each, we ordered dinner. Bill got the biggest steak on the menu. After a short deliberation, we all joined him and ordered steak with baked potatoes and salads. We each ordered one more beer and kept up our chatter until dinner arrived. Having been deprived of meat for the last week, we dove in head-first only to find the steak was tough as shoe leather. Still it was still a welcome change from the daily diet of fish. We all ordered dessert too, having developed a craving for ice cream somewhere between Wicksteed and Darky.

The meal wasn't great, but we didn't really care. We were all stuffed and ready to go back to our rooms and sleep in real beds with sheets. We paid our checks and walked out to find it was still raining lightly and felt thankful that we didn't have to pitch a tent or build another fire. We'd had a wonderful time but were ready to go home.

On our way back to the motel, we discussed the schedule for tomorrow. My flight wasn't until 1:20 and it was only a two-hour drive to Duluth. I'd called the airline earlier from the motel room and was told that they expected my flight to depart as scheduled. I was sure hoping that was true.

Knowing they had a long drive back to Chicago, I suggested that we get going early in the morning, have breakfast at the log cabin cafe, return our rented gear to the outfitter and hit the road. I had no problem killing time in the Duluth airport, so they could get a jump on their drive to Chicago.

Bill said we'd probably all be up by 6:00 anyway, since we'd been on that schedule all week. The first ones up would call the others and we'd get moving. The outfitter was open at 7:00 so we had plenty of time to eat breakfast, return our gear and hit the road. I'd have a few hours to kill at the airport, but the guys should be able to get home by evening.

Upon returning to our rooms, we retrieved our clothes from the dryer, packed our duffel bags and broke down our fishing gear for travel. We took the rented stuff to Wayne and Bill's room and piled it all together, then sat and talked for a little while longer.

When we started to yawn, Tom and I retired to our room, and crawled into clean sheets and real beds for the first time in more than a week. The last thing I remembered was looking at the clock radio which said 10:10.

Going Home

We awoke on Monday morning before the alarm went off. I had never been a natural early riser, but this week had been different. In Quetico I'd been physically tired every night because I had been physically active every day and had absolutely no trouble getting to sleep. Waking early was a result of going to bed early and sleeping soundly. I awoke refreshed nearly every morning on this trip, and vowed to try to keep this habit going, but feared it just wasn't in my genes. My dad had always been a "night person" and I felt doomed to that natural biorhythm. Time would tell.

Just as we had done eight days ago, Tom and I opened the door to see Wayne and Bill already packing the car. But this time we were heading home. Hauling our gear out the door, we piled it next to the car where Bill was trying to find a place for everything. The clouds had disappeared overnight, and the cool morning air was fresh from yesterday's rain. The sun was coming up behind the pines and I was looking forward to seeing my family before the day was done.

After packing, we checked out of the motel and headed to the log cabin café for breakfast. We tried to remember if it was Wednesday or Thursday that we ran out of eggs. I was pretty sure it was Wednesday. I looked forward to link sausage, two eggs over medium, hash browns, wheat toast with jelly, and fresh-brewed coffee. Everyone else had the same thing in mind with minor variations, but they all included eggs in one form or another.

Having seated ourselves at a window booth that looked out on the street, we commented on how the traffic seemed heavy for being so early. With Labor Day a month away, the town was still bustling. Our waitress brought coffee for all without even asking. We ordered right away, wanting to be at the outfitter shortly after 7:00 to turn in our equipment and get our deposits back. We didn't hurry our breakfast, wanting to savor it, but we didn't dawdle either.

Having finished, we paid our bills and were out the door by 7:15 and arrived at the outfitter ten minutes later. Taking our gear to the counter, one of the guys checked us in and returned our deposit. He asked how our trip went and we all concurred that it was terrific except for the Pond to Gratton portage. He laughed and said, "Nobody does that one twice unless they have to." We all agreed and said we would avoid that one in the future. We also told him that the campsite in Conmee that they'd recommended was top notch and thanked him for the tip.

Leaving the shop, we stepped out into the early Minnesota sunshine, taking a deep breath of the fresh pine air before getting back in the car and heading south. As we left town, I kind of knew I was leaving Ely for the last time. The further we got, the fewer signs we saw until we were back in the desolation of the Minnesota Northwoods. We passed a few lakes and streams that were void of human activity. It seemed a little odd seeing these beautiful, sparkling lakes from a car rather than a canoe.

As we drove, our conversation turned from the trip, back to our daily lives: family, jobs, sports, etc. As we got closer to Duluth, the road became busier and the billboards more frequent. Other signs of civilization began to appear, like gas stations, office buildings, and schools. Seeing a school reminded us that our kids would be back to school next month, right after Labor Day. Things were already starting to feel complicated again. Life was simple in Quetico, where we focused on food, shelter, and water.

Finally seeing a sign for the airport, Wayne, who was driving this leg, followed the directions to the terminal, pulling up to the curb at about 10:15. We all got out to stretch. When Bill packed this morning, he wisely put my stuff in last, so we wouldn't need to dig for it. We all stood there a bit awkwardly. This really marked the end of the trip, where we split up. We floated the idea of Mary Jane and I coming over to Chicago for a weekend sometime in the next few months to relive the trip with a slide show. That made the split a little easier. It wasn't really "good-bye," it was more like, "see you in a couple of months". With that we all shook hands, I picked up my duffel and fishing rod case, turned and headed for the entrance. I didn't turn around for fear that they would see I had something in my eye.

Walking up to the ticket counter, I checked my duffle and rod case. The agent stapled the baggage claim stubs to my ticket envelope and I was free for the next three hours. I found a bank of pay phones and called home. Mary Jane answered on the second ring… it was good to hear her voice again. I told her where I was, and about our dinner last night, and I asked about the boys.

She said they had all spent most of the weekend over at her parents' house. They only lived about twenty minutes away in a little brick house in the country with five acres and a small pond. Jamie, the oldest, had caught twelve frogs on Sunday and his little brother, Tim, had caught four. They put the frogs in Granddad's old galvanized minnow bucket for an hour or so, then they all made a big production of going out to the end of the short dock and letting them go, shrieking with delight as they jumped back in the pond. Granddad kept track of who caught what on a little chalkboard in the shed.

We said goodbye and I told her I should be home before 6:00. I lost an hour going back to Eastern Time. I hung up the phone and went to explore this little airport terminal. There wasn't much here. It was even smaller than the terminal in Lansing where I'd had to kill a couple of hours on my way up here. I bought a newspaper, found some coffee and sat awhile, trying to catch up on the week's news. I wandered the terminal, end-to-end, went outside and walked for some exercise, then came back and did the crossword puzzle. It was a long time to kill without much to do. There was very little air traffic in or out of Duluth on a Monday morning in August.

Finally, at about 12:30 I went and sat at the gate. A few people began to wander into the gate area and the agent showed up a little before 1:00 and began checking us in. I'd been half-holding my breath, fearing they might still cancel the flight because of the strike, but when we began boarding, I finally relaxed and felt certain that I was going to get home. The flight was only about half-full, so I got a window seat again, this time just behind the left wing.

Departing the gate, the flight attendant went through the safety ritual, with barely anyone paying attention. We taxied out and took off to the west, and after reaching a safe altitude, began a gradual left turn.

Finally, I could see the sun glinting off Lake Superior to my left as we settled into a southeast heading towards Lansing. Staring off into the hazy distance, once again flying over the forests of northern Wisconsin, I recalled the camping trip from eight or nine years ago, when Mary Jane and I got chased from the shore of Trout Lake onto a small island by a skunk.

I was in a melancholy mood as we crossed the Lake Michigan shoreline, this time north of Green Bay. We made Michigan landfall just north of Traverse City, over Sleeping Bear Dunes and the Leelanau Peninsula, one of my favorite places on earth. Quetico Provincial Park had been added to that short list this week. About twenty minutes later, we were beginning our descent into Lansing. We touched down on-time and as we taxied to the gate, I was thankful that the PATCO strike had not had any effect on my trip, other than causing me some anxiety.

After a brief wait for my duffel and rod case, I walked the 200-300 yards to my car. I recalled a little more than a week ago making that walk, trying to pretend it was a portage. It was absolutely *nothing* like a portage! I knew so little then.

I made the 45-minute drive home enjoying the perfect summer weather. When I arrived, I was met enthusiastically by Mary Jane and the kids. Simultaneously, they started asking me all kinds of questions. I gave them all a big hug and said, "Let's go inside and I'll tell you all about it."

Epilogue

I've thought about this trip countless times over the last thirty plus years. It came at a wonderful time in my life, when I was still young enough to handle the physical demands. Although the trip we took was physically challenging in places, there are lots of other routes that one could take that are much less so.

There are many parts of the Boundary Waters Canoe Area (BWCA), on the Minnesota side that are open to day trips and short overnight stays that will still give one the sense of adventure and wilderness experience that I had. The Canadian side and the US side are indistinguishable and are equally beautiful and wild. The border really doesn't exist anywhere except in some cryptic international documents hidden away in the bureaucratic bowels of Ottawa or Washington. Nature has no regard for a line on a map. Nor do the eagles, otters, beavers, moose, or fish.

When I look back, I'm still awed by the beauty and solitude we enjoyed. I expected that part, and never got tired of it, nor did I ever take it for granted. I expected to catch a lot of fish and I surely wasn't disappointed. The things I didn't expect or foresee are some of the fondest memories of all for me. I wasn't expecting the magnificent stargazing and satellite counting. I wasn't expecting the reverence I felt while looking at the pictographs, or the spirituality of watching a Bald Eagle perched high above us in the top of a white pine. These things *moved* me.

Though not a regular churchgoer, I have a simple faith and belief in God. Nature is my church; the woods and water, the sky and the earth itself. I feel it in my soul. I see the diversity of the natural world and wonder how anyone can believe that it was all just an accident, a big bang. If it was, where did the very first spark of life come from? What *is* life? These are questions as old as humanity itself and many philosophers, much wiser than me, have struggled and anguished over them for countless generations. I can only speak for myself.

Studying wildlife and natural resource management in college, I learned much about evolution. The concept is undeniable... that species *do* evolve and *do* adapt as conditions, climate, food supplies, and environments change. I believe that evolution occurs *within* species, not *between* species. I cannot get my head around the argument that *all* life evolved from a single cell that started it all. There's way too much variety and diversity in flora and fauna for me to buy it.

Nature is highlighted in places like Quetico and BWCA, where it is inescapable. It *is* nature because *there is no* distraction or escape from it. Literally, besides what we brought with us, the *only* man-made objects we saw for eight days, were the passenger jet we saw at 30,000 feet flying over us on the first evening, and the satellites.

I would urge anyone who has the desire and the opportunity to make a trip like this in their lifetime to just go for it. You'll not be disappointed!

Acknowledgements

Both thanks and apologies go to Mary Jane for putting up with my mental absence over the countless hours I've spent at my computer anguishing over this story when I should have been taking out the garbage or cleaning up dog poop in the yard.

I especially want to express my sincere gratitude to my good friend, Tom Newman, who by his invitation, made this adventure happen for me. Also, many thanks to Tom's brothers-in-law, Wayne Thomas and Bill Hare, both of whom welcomed me on this adventure with open arms despite my inexperience. Together, among a host of other things, they patiently taught me how to get a canoe on my back without killing myself.

Both of my sons are professional writers and helped me immeasurably. My love and thanks to them both; Tim for his superb copy-editing expertise and Jamie for his proofreading skills.

A very special thanks to Jenny Harley, an amazing graphic artist who somehow found a way to sum up this entire trip in a single image, which is the beautiful cover art for this book.

Finally, to you, the reader, I hope you enjoyed the trip as much as I did. Regardless, I would very much appreciate you leaving an honest review on either Amazon or Goodreads.

William Monger
November 2019